BEYOND BELIEF

INCREDIBLE STORIES OF OLD ST. JOHN'S

JACK FITZGERALD

Books by Jack Fitzgerald available through Creative:

Jack Fitzgerald's Notebook
Amazing Newfoundland Stories
Newfoundland Fireside Stories
Another Time, Another Place
The Hangman is Never Late

BEYOND BELIEF

INCREDIBLE STORIES OF OLD ST. JOHN'S

JACK FITZGERALD

CREATIVE PUBLISHERS
St. John's, Newfoundland
2001

Le Conseil des Arts | The Canada Council
du Canada | for the Arts

We acknowledge the support of The Canada Council for the Arts for our
publishing program.

We acknowledge the financial support of the Government of Canada through the
Book Publishing Industry Development Program (BPIDP) for our
publishing program.

Cover Art and Design: Maurice Fitzgerald

∞ Printed on acid-free paper

Published by
CREATIVE BOOK PUBLISHING
a division of 10366 Newfoundland Limited
a Robinson-Blackmore Printing & Publishing associated company
P.O. Box 8660, St. John's, Newfoundland A1B 3T7

First Printing — July 2001
Second Printing — September 2001
Third Printing — April 2002

Printed in Canada by:
ROBINSON-BLACKMORE PRINTING & PUBLISHING

National Library of Canada Cataloguing in Publication Data

Fitzgerald, Jack, 1945–
    Beyond belief: incredible stories of old St. John's

ISBN 1-894294-31-9

    1. St. John's (Nfld.)— History—Ancedotes.   I. Title

FC2196.36.F58   2001   971.8'1   C2001-901882-7
F1124.5.S 1 4F58   2001

Contents

INTRODUCTION

Beyond Belief brings together under one cover some of the most incredible and intriguing stories ever collected of old St. John's. Some of these stories have not been previously published, but most have been gleaned from the other fifteen books I have written since 1980.

By collecting these stories into one book the reader has ready access to the incredible side of St. John's long history. In addition to providing interesting reading, I feel Beyond Belief will be a valuable aid to both residents and visitors to the city. From this book the reader can organize a variety of tours of the city for personal enjoyment, or to entertain friends and visitors. With topics taken from the macabre, curious and incredible Beyond Belief will be a valuable aid to those wanting to promote the colourful history of old St. John's.

St. John's has, unfortunately, lost most of its physical history through fire, carelessness and neglect. Beyond Belief is one step in making sure the many stories that contribute to the colour and mystic of our St. John's heritage do not meet the same fate.

—Jack Fitzgerald
June, 2001

BURIED TREASURE

Stories of buried treasure have been around as long as the earth has been populated. Due to its location, Newfoundland has it's fair share of treasure stories. Here are a few from the St. John's area.

JOHN KEATING'S SECRET
Originally appeared in *Jack Fitzgerald's Notebook*

John Keating's secret was connected with a $70,000,000 treasure stolen from a group of people in Lima, Peru. When Simon Bolivar led his forces from the hillsides of Peru towards the country's capital at Lima, authorities in Lima were in a panic. Concerned that Bolivar would steal the treasures of the city, they hatched a plan to smuggle out of the country gold and jewellery worth over $70,000,000 dollars.

However, Bolivar was approaching the city too fast for the proper arrangements to be made, so they rushed the fortune to the Lima waterfront, hoping to find a trustworthy person to take it out of the country for safe keeping. In desperation they entrusted the treasure to a Newfoundland sea captain named Captain William Thompson, of the brig *Mary Dear*. But they picked the wrong man! Thompson sailed out of Lima and the Peruvians never saw their treasure again.

Meanwhile, Thompson buried the treasure on Cocos Island and returned to hide out in Newfoundland. While in St. John's he befriended a ship's carpenter named John

Keating and told him of the treasure. He had hoped that Keating would help him retrieve the stolen goods. Governor LeMarchant learned that Thompson, who was wanted by British authorities for piracy, was in the city and Thompson narrowly escaped capture. The Peruvians and British authorities were searching all over America for him. He escaped St. John's on foot and his body was later found in a bank of snow near Bay Bulls, where he had died of exposure. Legend has it, however, that the Peruvian Indians had placed a curse on him.

John Keating developed a partnership with a Captain Boag, and the duo set out to find the Cocos treasure. When the crew saw the treasure they mutinied. Captain Boag filled his pockets with gold and jumped into a dory, which capsized. The weight of the gold dragged him under and he drowned. Keating took his share and made it back to St. John's. He never returned to seek the remainder of the treasure but, before he passed away, he told of its existence and location to two people. During the 1840s he became shipwrecked in the St. Lawrence River and was rescued by Captain Nick Fitzgerald of Harbour Grace. In gratitude for the rescue he told Fitzgerald of the treasure. Shortly after returning to St. John's he became ill and died. Before his death he also told his daughter, Mrs. Richard Young, of the treasure's location.

Captain Fitzgerald formed a company with retired British Admiral Hugh Palliser to search for the gold, while Keating's daughter teamed up with German explorer Van Brewer to seek it — if they found any of the treasure, it was never revealed. Word of the Cocos treasure spread and so many attempts were made to find it that the Costa Rican Government implemented a $1000 per month treasure hunting fee at Cocos.

SIGNAL HILL GOLD

When the British drove the French — for the final time — from Signal Hill in St. John's during the eighteenth century, the French were forced to leave behind a fortune in gold. The French Garrison had imported the gold to pay its soldiers and purchase supplies for its forces. They carried with them what they could, and the remainder was buried somewhere on Signal Hill. There was speculation it was buried near the old Blockhouse (now Cabot Tower) area.

During August 1921, the city was swept with excitement after word spread that the French gold had been found. People swarmed to the area and discovered an open and freshly dug hole about ten feet deep.

Rumours spread that the keeper of the Blockhouse had found the money. This conjecture was fuelled by the fact that soon after the rumours started, the caretaker quit his job and moved to the United States.

During the 1920s Ronald Lacey, who had moved to the United States with his family as a child, returned to St. John's on a visit. Lacey told friends of a family friend in Brooklyn named Miller who had once worked as keeper at the Blockhouse on Signal Hill. Miller was then a wealthy man, and claimed he had found a fortune in gold before leaving Newfoundland. Lacey recalled that Miller only talked about the gold when he had too much to drink. He was surprised when he learned the story of the hidden French gold on Signal Hill. He told his friends that Miller had insisted that he only removed half of the treasure, and hoped one day to come back for the remainder.

Miller passed away a few years later, but enough of the story was then known to inspire many city residents to go treasure hunting on Signal Hill. However, there are no records of any more of the gold having been found.

TREASURE IN THE GRAVE

Little Bell Island, a couple of miles from St. John's, is the site of another intriguing story of hidden treasure. In 1862 Captain Mark Delaney, a Newfoundlander, met with an old seaman while in port at Lisbon, Portugal, and learned of a treasure in gold coins buried at Little Bell Island, Conception Bay.

The old seaman was delighted to learn that Delaney was from St. John's. He told the captain that he had lived the life of a pirate and had visited Newfoundland many times. One visit that stood out in memory was an incident in which his ship was pursued by a British-man-o'-war.

To avoid being caught with the stolen treasure, they pulled into Little Bell Island where the pirates put their gold in an iron chest, and then into a box made of oak. Then it was buried, leaving a mound of earth as though a recent funeral had taken place. The pirates then raised a similar mound on each side to give the appearance of three graves. When finished they left the island. The old pirate said the British caught up with them and only a few escaped. He was one of the few. What happened to the others he did not know and he never returned to seek the treasure. He told Delaney he had stored enough gold during his career to make him a wealthy man.

When Delaney returned to St. John's he visited the island to seek the treasure. Using the marks and tokens given him by the old pirate, he found the graves. Because there were other fishermen on the island he chose not to dig but to come back at a later time when he felt the area would be deserted.

When he returned he found the graves had been opened, and were empty. Nearby he found fragments of an iron bound oak chest which he kept as a souvenir. He later learned that while he was away two strangers had come to Topsail, purchased a punt and rowed to the island. They visited a short while and left, never to be seen again. The boat was found abandoned near Topsail several days later. In the bottom of the boat were several gold coins.

OXEN POND GOLD

According to city folklore, a strongbox of gold lies hidden beneath the waters of Oxen Pond in the north of St. John's. The pond derived its name from a British soldier Lieutenant J. Oxenham who served in St. John's during the late eighteenth century. In that era control of St. John's changed hands between the English and the French on many occasions.

To protect St. John's against a surprise French attack, British soldiers manned sentry posts throughout Victoria Hills in the Oxen Pond area. Lieutenant Oxenham, accompanied by an armed guard, set out to deliver wages to the soldiers on duty when they were attacked by French soldiers advancing towards St. John's.

Oxenham attempted to escape by running down a path carrying with him the strongbox of gold. However, he was trapped on the shore of the pond. Before being taken prisoner by the French he tossed the box of gold as far as he could out into the pond. When the French caught up with him they had no idea about the gold and simply took him to their garrison at Placentia.

Over the ensuing decades many soldiers searched unsuccessfully for the treasure. The last known search was made by several Broadcove fishermen in the 1920s. If they found any of the gold they kept their secret well.

According to the story, the British named the pond Oxenham Pond after the Lieutenant in appreciation for his effort to keep the gold out of French hands. Over the years the name of the pond was shortened to Oxen Pond.

THE PIRATE GHOST OF QUIDI VIDI

In the early 1800s a pirate vessel, attempting to evade capture by the British Navy, pulled into Quidi Vidi Harbour. The pirates carted a treasure of silver and gold to a site adjacent to Quidi Vidi Lake and buried it, with the intention of returning during safer times to recover it.

In 1820, one of the pirates returned to claim the gold for himself. While in St. John's he stayed at the home of a Mr. O'Regan, who operated a shoe store in the city's west end. However, before he could get a chance to search for the treasure he became gravely ill and passed away. Before the man died, Father Forestall was called to the home by Mr. O'Regan. The dying man's confession was heard, and last rites administered. In appreciation for O'Regan's Christian kindness the dying man confessed to his friend that he had been a pirate and he gave him a map showing where at Quidi Vidi the pirates had hidden their gold.

The map described Bennett's Grove adjacent to Quidi Vidi Lake in the vicinity of Dribbling Brook (east of the boathouse). The place to dig was thirty paces west of the brook. O'Regan employed several fishermen from Quidi Vidi Village — William Quigley, Richard Mallard and William Smithwick — to help him dig for the gold and silver. The trio spent three days digging without any success when O'Regan ordered them to stop their digging. O'Regan had discovered the buried treasure and planned to remove it himself. However, he had not anticipated that another group was already heading for Bennett's Grove to seek the treasure.

A small group headed by Kenneth Connors worked at night to avoid arousing suspicion. While working one night, an eerie cry rang out through the area. The cry startled the men and one commented, "It's the cry of the Banshee." Around the same time a misty figure began moving slowly towards the men and waving a sword over his head. Ken Connors had a heart attack and dropped dead. Another man ran from the area screaming. Days later he was still in shock and eventually was admitted to the Asylum where he spent the rest of his days.

By the time Ken Connors was buried, there was not a non-believer of ghosts in town. However, as the treasure story became known, speculation grew that O'Regan had disguised himself as a phantom pirate with sword, to scare the treasure seekers from his dig. O'Regan, left a few months later to settle in the United States, and the local people believed he had taken a portion — if not all — of the Quidi Vidi treasure with him.

The treasure fever — and ghost story — faded from public memory until a little over a decade later when a stranger arrived in St. John's on board the SS *Florizel*. The man, from Boston, sought and received permission from the Honourable A.M. Mackay to dig on his property at Dribbling Brook. Mr. Eddie, who operated a coal yard on Carter's Hill, befriended the stranger and sometimes helped with the digging.

Mr. Eddie learned from the stranger that a man named O'Regan had passed away in Boston, and before dying had given him the treasure map. Although the American placed some trust in Mr. Eddie, he would withdraw into the woods whenever others approached him.

Then one morning at daylight a resident of the area saw the American row a boat up from the foot of the lake to the cove near where he was digging, and lift on board a large box from the grove. The stranger then rowed back to the end of the lake where he loaded the box onto a horse and buggy and drove away. The resident went to the grove but found only an empty hole with about eight feet of clay piled up along its side.

By this time Dribbling Brook had changed direction and the stranger had searched for the treasure on the dried up river-bed, that a hundred years earlier had been Dribbling Brook. Meanwhile, Mr. Eddie was not ready to give up and he was convinced there was some treasure still in the area. His belief was based on information he picked up from the visitor that one man could not carry all the treasure hidden near the brook.

Mr. Eddy formed a group which included the Honourable Mackay and Thomas Kent of Quidi Vidi. They agreed to share the treasure equally and to pay diggers one dollar per day to do the digging for them. After seven days of unsuccessful digging the project was called off. Rumours spread that one of the diggers had found some gold coins and kept them. Mackay and his group felt there was still a sizeable treasure in the area, but because the brook had changed direction they could never locate it.

Well into the 1950s many people of the city felt that Bennett's Grove was haunted and would avoid that area after dark.

JUSTICE FAIR AND FOUL

In the early days of Newfoundland's colonization, justice was both swift and harsh. As time passed both the courts and the law itself became more sophisticated. Here are a few stories of Justice as it was applied in St. John's from the early days to the past century.

QUIDI VIDI MURDER

Originally appeared in *The Hangman is Never Late*

On September 9, 1754, the community of Quidi Vidi Village was the scene of a commando-type robbery and murder. The victim, William Kean, was a prominent Newfoundland court justice whom the attackers believed had a fortune hidden in his summer home at Quidi Vidi.

The group included nine men and one woman and became known in criminal history as the 'Power Gang,' with Eleanor Power, who dressed in men's clothing for the attack, as leader. The original plan did not include murder. Two members of the gang entered the house at night while the others remained on guard outside. Inside the house the two found Kean's bedroom and, while he slept, removed a large box from beneath his bed. During the robbery Judge Kean awoke and began shouting, "Murder, Murder!" Kean struggled with the robbers who retaliated with a scythe and the butt of a gun. The next morning the community of St. John's was shocked to learn of the raid on Kean's property and of his murder.

In less than a month, through the help of one of the gang members, all ten were arrested, convicted and sentenced to be hanged. The man who informed on the others was released. Five other members who had not entered the house and did not participate in the murder were pardoned. Eleanor Power, her husband Richard, and the remaining two participants were hanged from a gallows constructed in the area now occupied by the Royal Trust Building on Water Street. All four were buried near the gallows.

ANOTHER CRIME AT QUIDI VIDI
Originally appeared in Jack Fitzgerald's Notebook

During 1759 William Gilmore operated a successful business in his home in Quidi Vidi Village, selling liquor to soldiers from the Garrison in St. John's. During April of the same year, Gilmore was executed at Gallows Hill (corner Queen's Road and Bate's Hill) by hanging, for his part in the stealing of a cow.

Gilmore had encouraged two friends to kill one of the cows grazing in a meadow in the area now occupied by Government House. He planned the crime and arranged to hide the meat in his well.

The duo killed the cow but left the knife given to them by Gilmore at the scene of the crime. Authorities found the knife, and Gilmore's wife identified it as her husband's. Justice was swift, and within days the trial and execution had been completed. Historical records are not clear on what happened to the two young men who did the bidding of William Gilmore.

In the eighteenth century there were more than 122 crimes for which a person could be executed. One of these was the stealing of a cow.

HANGED AT FORT TOWNSHEND

Originally appeared in Jack Fitzgerald's Notebook

John Pelley of Bonne Bay was hanged on the gallows at Fort Townshend during September of 1809. Pelley had been tried in court at St. John's and found guilty of double murder. His victims were Joe Randell and Richard Cross, who had both shared a hunting lodge with him at Shallow Cove.

Cross's sister, Sarah Singleton, had complained to police after becoming alarmed over the disappearance of her brother and Joe Randell. Authorities organized a search for the missing men while Sarah and a neighbour John Paine stayed the night at Pelley's house. Early next morning they joined in the search and, finding some items of clothing belonging to her brother, Sarah cried out, 'Oh God, my brother has been murdered."

Paine shared her view but cautioned her saying, "Hold your tongue, Pelley is not far away and if he hears you he may come and kill us."

Sarah and John returned to Rocky Harbour and enlisted the help of three friends. They returned to confront Pelley with an accusation of murder. The confession was extracted in a way that no court today with accept. They built a large fire and kept forcing Pelley closer to it until he confessed.

Pelley was kept locked up in a private home at Bonne Bay until arrangements were completed to transfer him to St. John's for trial. While a prisoner, Pelley shed some light on the double murders saying, "It all started when Randell told me to go out and cut some wood, I grumbled about it and said, '...if you don't keep quiet, I'll knock your liver out.' He came at me and I killed him with an ax."

Cross witnessed the killing and told Pelley, "You wouldn't kill me would you?" But Pelley said he ignored Cross's plea and axed him to death, also. Justice Tom Tremblett sentenced Pelley to be hanged. On the day of the execution he was tied to a horse-drawn cart which paraded him through the streets of St. John's. The execution procession ended at Fort Townshend where a gallows had been erected.

Pelley was escorted up the gallows where the masked executioner placed a white hood over his head. The crowd moved closer as the executioner dropped the noose over the condemned man, and stepped back to release the trapdoor. The noose tightened quickly around Pelley's neck and death was instant. It was a spectacle long remembered by the people of St. John's.

DEADMAN'S POND — SIGNAL HILL

Deadman's Pond, near the Tourist Interpretation Centre on Signal Hill, got its name during the eighteenth century when a hill near the pond was used for public executions. In some criminal cases the Courts would add gibbeting to the sentence of hanging. This meant that the executed felon would have the added indignity of being left hanging in chains for days after the execution as a reminder to others of the consequences of violating the law.

In time, as the corpse decayed and the odour became offensive, the body would be cut down. It was then stuffed in a barrel with several holes in it and partly filled with stones. This made the burial process easy. The funeral consisted simply of rolling the barrel down the hill and into the nearby pond where it sank to the bottom.

The pond is not as deep today as it was in the eighteenth century due to infilling over the years. But it remains to this day the burial site of several executed criminals. From this practice came the name Deadman's Pond and the nearby hill is still called Gibbet's Hill.

THE SCROOGE OF WATER STREET
Originally appeared in *Newfoundland Fireside Stories*

Buried at the General Protestant Cemetery in St. John's is Archibald Sillars, remembered in Newfoundland criminal history as the Scrooge of Water Street. A peculiar gravestone marks the burial site of Sillars, who is buried just sixty feet from the west gate on Waterford Bridge Road. The tombstone lies horizontal on the grave and bears his name, date of death and place of birth. There are several other similar tombstones in St. John's. One marks the grave of the eccentric Professor Charles Danielle in the Church of England Cemetery on Forest Road.

Sillars was shot and beaten to death in a basement office of a Water Street establishment he had sold to

The grave of Archibald Sillars, General Protestant Cemetery, St. John's.

13

William Parnell. Sillars had guaranteed part of the loan raised by Parnell to purchase the general store. However, after the sale he visited the store regularly and harassed customers of Parnell who owed Sillars money. He also tormented Parnell, his wife and children. When Parnell found it difficult to make the required payments on his loans, Sillars threatened to toss him and his family on the street. Christmas was approaching and the threat placed much stress and torment on the shoulders of Parnell.

On the night of November 30, the two argued over money, and Parnell accused Sillars of sticking him with useless goods that couldn't be sold. In the heat of argument he pulled a revolver and fired three bullets into Sillars. Sillars crawled towards the stairway but Parnell picked up a shovel and beat Sillars over the head until he was dead.

Parnell then went to his upstairs bedroom and took poison. However, he was revived by a doctor, and when the facts surrounding the murder surfaced, he was arrested and tried for murder.

Parnell was found guilty of murder and executed at Her Majesty's penitentiary on July 8, 1889.

This marked one of several bungled hangings in Newfoundland history. Parnell was a heavy-set man and the inexperienced executioner allowed for a rope that was too long. When Parnell fell through the gallows the rope almost completely severed his head.

THE MURDER OF ENG WING KIT

Originally appeared in *The Hangman is Never Late*

During the 1940s and early 1950s many people would get the cold shivers late at night while passing a house near the crossroads on Water Street West, where one of the most bizarre murders in Newfoundland history took place.

The house was once the home of Eng Wing Kit and two partners, who also operated the Regal Cafe from that address. Kit's body was discovered on the morning of July 3, 1938 by Kilbride farmer Gordon Stanley. The press described it as a ceremonial killing. The victim had been found with a rope around his neck and tied to an iron pipe laid across the kitchen table and stove. His throat had been cut and a circular piece of flesh cut from his chest. Acting on tips given by members of the Chinese community, police arrested Quang John Shang who hailed from the same village in China as the victim.

A sensational trial followed in which Shang was acquitted. Soon after the trial he left Newfoundland and never returned. Shang died in the 1990s in British Columbia. The murder of Eng Wing Kit has never been solved. Kit is buried in the General Protestant Cemetery on Waterford Bridge Road.

THINGS THAT GO BUMP IN THE NIGHT

Newfoundland has a rich and interesting history
in things paranormal. Documentation of unusual
and supernatural events form part of our early
history, and continue to the present day. Here are a
number of unique stories pertaining to St. John's
and its environs. Some of the stories in this chapter
involve murder and its aftermath, so make a natural extension to the previous chapter.

RAINBOW

Originally appeared in *Strange but True Newfoundland Stories*

On March 25th, 1842 a phenomena occurred in the skies
over St. John's which prompted Newfoundland historian,
Lord Bonnycastle, to record the event in his book *History
of Newfoundland.*

He recorded that he was a witness to an unusual
appearance, a bow that was not a rainbow, nor displaying
ordinary colours of a rainbow. He wrote,

> On the evening of Good Friday, March 25th, 1842,
> with the thermometer at 30 degrees Fahrenheit and
> a North-east wind, a most unusual appearance was
> exhibited at sunset around 6:30 p.m.
>   The western sky over St. John's was a blaze of
> rosette and fire coloured angry light after the sun
> dipped, a blaze which reflected on the eastern or sea
> sky to a great extent; and just as the sun had disap-
> peared behind the hill, a perfect bow appeared in the
> east. This bow did not have the usual rainbow colours.

It was made up of a variation of the colour red, from fiery red to the Rosette.

Bonnycastle noted that the phenomena was a perfect arch of the usual size and height of a rainbow at sunset. He added that the previous evening the eastern sky at sunset was beautifully coloured with purple and red down to the horizon, while the western sky was not. The thermometer varied only two or three degrees above or below freezing all the time; yet both these appearances were succeeded only by light thaws.

The historian wrote that while snow covered the land and ice lay off shore, there was neither snow nor rain during the two days of the unusual phenomena. Some people thought it was the end of the world. The unusual rainbow of 1842 was never explained.

Because it happened on Good Friday people of the city felt it had a religious significance and the churches were filled to capacity.

THREE SUNS OVER ST. JOHN'S
Originally appeared in *Jack Fitzgerald's Notebook*

One of the most unusual natural phenomena to occur in Newfoundland happened during the mid-nineteenth century when three suns appeared over the island. The sight was visible all over St. John's.

David King, a fisherman, described the event in his diary. He wrote:

The previous night to the apparition or whatever you want to call it, it froze very hard and the weather gave every indication of a hard frost. Very little coal was used by people and we used to go the woods for our fuel. On the morning when the three suns appeared the wind veered to the North with snow flurries and by 10 a.m. a miserable day was in progress. At 11:15 the sky cleared temporarily and visible to all our population was three separate suns shining down from the heavens. Some people took this as a sign the world was going to end and the Churches were filled with people saving their souls. But then the clouds came again and the three suns were no longer visible. It got cold, very, very cold. Jim Kielley, who kept a store on Water Street put outside his door a bucket of water and in just five minutes the water was frozen solid. It got so cold that people on the roads had to take shelter in nearby houses.

Captain Patrick Spry painted a picture of the city of St. John's with the three suns over it and it was left on display in the windows of Bowrings Store for many years.

Historian H.M. Mosdell recorded in his book *What Year Was That?* That the phenomena of three suns over St. John's occurred on February 26, 1840 and again on March 7, 1904.

THE CURE

Modern medicine has eradicated many of the diseases faced by our ancestors. In addition, new vaccines have been developed to prevent measles and many other childhood diseases. However, at the turn of the century in St. John's, many parents had little faith in doctors and medicine. In those days it was commonly believed that children suffering from whooping cough, measles, croup and other sicknesses could be cured by uttering the name of the Blessed Trinity as the child was passed three times beneath and over the back of an ass that had the mark of the crucifix on its back.

Mary Evoy, who passed away in 1950 at the age of seventy-eight, recalled the belief and explained it was an

Irish superstition based on the story in the Bible of an ass carrying the Virgin Mary into Bethlehem. Mary said that Bill Dawe, who operated a small farm near St. John's, made more money using this technique than some of the St. John's doctors. Bill, at the time, owned the only ass in eastern Newfoundland, which had a white cross on its back. At one time, when an epidemic of measles raged throughout the city, Dawe set up business at Solomon's Lane. People stood in line, their infants clutched in their arms, waiting for Bill Dawe to administer the blessed cure.

SHOWER OF BLOOD

Joe Hepditch of Goodridge Street in St. John's spent many years fishing with crews on the Grand Banks. One particular trip which became emblazoned in his memory, and one which he told and retold over the years, took place in 1890. Hepditch said, "I thought the end of the world was at hand." He was referring to a phenomena which was reported in American newspapers, and spooked all the fishermen in the area where it occurred.

Hepditch said he was working with several other men on deck when the sea suddenly became very calm and the skies darkened. The change was so sudden that the entire crew took notice, and work on other vessels in the area also stopped as crew members stood in wonder. Hepditch told friends that, "suddenly it began to pour and at first we thought it was raining. Then we noticed it was raining blood." The oddity lasted several minutes and then stopped. When Hepditch returned to his home in St. John's he told family and friends. There was no explanation for the event and the bewildered men who had witnessed concluded it was a warning of a pending disaster.

Another ship in the area, under the command of Captain Michael Trennery, was on its way to Baltimore via the Grand Banks when the curiosity struck. He recalled the sudden change in weather and the calming of the sea, "...it seemed something unusual was to take place." Crew men were frightened and began praying aloud.

Trennery explained what happened next,

> Off the Newfoundland Banks a phenomena was witnessed, it being nothing more or less than a rain of blood apparently, and covered the decks, bridge, masts, stocks, boats and every exposed part.
>
> When it came down it was a dark rich colour like human blood, but soon dried up and assumed the colour of dust. All hands were scared and feared a serious accident would happen."

Trennery also felt it was a warning of a pending disaster. Others who reported seeing the Shower of Blood included Captain John Inch and the crew of the Rossmore.

When Trennery arrived at Baltimore he revealed the story to a newspaper reporter and the report was carried in many major newspapers throughout the United States. Trennery commented, "It was a truly remarkable and frightening sight." Scientists questioned by reporters could offer no explanation for the phenomena.

However Hepditch didn't need any scientific explanation. He believed the event was a warning of disaster. Two years later he was confirmed in his belief when in 1892 fire destroyed most of St. John's. Over later decades people in the area who retold the story described the Shower of Blood as an omen forecasting the disaster that struck St. John's.

REGATTA DAY EARTHQUAKE

An earthquake, which was felt from Signal Hill to Victoria Street, struck St. John's on the morning of Regatta Day, July 1898. The day after the event the following article appeared in the *Evening Telegram* (July 28,1898).

Did anyone notice a trembling, as if an earthquake, at seven o'clock on the morning of the Regatta? At that hour the signalman on the Block House, Michael Cantwell, having just hoisted the colours announcing the steamer Iceland was arriving when he certainly felt the whole structure vibrate and a noise as if a sudden gust of wind had struck and shook the place.

He walked out of the apartment and looked up at the Flag. It was hanging idly up and down the mast, and scarcely a breath stirred the atmosphere. Wondering what the matter could have been he went back into the room, and was no sooner there than the phenomena occurred a second time.

He finds it difficult to explain the strange occurrence except upon the hypothesis of it being two shocks of earthquake. So far, as is known, nothing of the kind was experienced in the town. The motions continued for about two seconds each, and there were about twenty seconds between each occurrence."

After reading the *Telegram* story, several residents in the Victoria Street area reported they had felt the quake and in one case it caused a house to tremble.

QUEEN OF THE DEAD

Nancy Coyle was an unusual woman with an unusual occupation which earned her the title of Queen of the Dead, and inspired bizarre stories about her; some claiming she could bring back the dead.

During the 1840s Nancy lived in a cottage surrounded

by a beautiful garden, located at the eastern corner of Carter's Hill and Queen's Road. During this period in St. John's history the city had no morgue. The government contracted with Nancy Coyle to look after the unidentified and unclaimed dead in addition to those foreign seaman who died accidentally or otherwise while in port.

A horse-drawn springless cart, which served as an ambulance from the hospital at Victoria Park on Water Street West, (then Riverhead) was also used to carry the dead. This wagon was frequently seen coming and going from Coyle's picturesque cottage. Nancy's job was to clean and dress the dead and to have them placed in a coffin for burial.

On several occasions incidents happened in the home which contributed to Nancy being recognized as a legendary figure of old St. John's for half a century. On at least one occasion a man who had been prepared for burial and was being nailed into a coffin moved and made moaning sounds. Nancy poured a drink of rum and revived him. On several other occasions people thought to be dead sat up while being prepared for burial. When these stories became known among the local population Nancy became known as the Queen of the Dead. By the turn of the twentieth century parents would tell their children stories of the Queen of the Dead, sometimes described as a witch, who brought the dead back to life. Children were told to avoid the area of the old residence of Nancy Coyle.

The original residence was destroyed by fire and replaced with a new home which was torn down during the urban renewal of the 1960s.

THE BELVEDERE HEARSE

Jack Adams, who worked for more than twenty years with CBC Television, told me of a strange incident he and a co-worker witnessed one morning at Belvedere Cemetery. It was about 5:30 on a sunny June morning when they were driving to work along Newtown Road.

As they approached Belvedere they were amazed to see a hearse moving in their direction take a left turn and go into the cemetery. While they had seen many funerals, this one had an uncanny aspect to it. It wasn't a motor driven hearse, but a horse-drawn carriage, with a driver in silks and high hat holding a black whip in one hand. Also there was no procession following the hearse.

The duo drove slowly past the open gate with their eyes glued to the hearse as it moved cautiously down the cemetery path. When it stopped just past mid-way Jack and his friend decided to pull into the side of the road and watch was happening. At first they thought that a theatre

Courtesy of Carnell's Funeral Home

A common sight when this photo was taken in 1947, the horse-drawn hearse went out of service in the early 1950s, and was only a distant memory at the time of this story.

24

group in the city might be putting together some kind of film. They exited the vehicle and walked to the gate. In the few seconds it took to park and walk the few feet to the open gate the black hearse had disappeared.

The two men searched all over the cemetery but could not find any sign of the hearse.

They returned to their car and continued on to work totally baffled and amazed by what they had seen.

THE PRESERVED CORPSE

Some years after hearing Jack Adams' story I talked with a retired gravedigger who, upon hearing the tale, told me another interesting event which took place at Belvedere Cemetery. He said he was working alone digging a grave, near the site where Jack Adams saw the strange looking black hearse. There was another body in the grave which had been buried decades before. In cases like this the grave digger was always alert so as not to disturb the buried corpse. He was astonished to uncover the remains of a lady, rosary beads in hand and the body as fresh as the day it was put in the grave, although the casket had almost entirely rotted away.

The man sought out his supervisor and brought him to the open grave to view the find. The supervisor said he had never witnessed anything like it. They then decided that this matter should be brought to the attention of the Bishop. The next day the grave digger was told by his boss that the Bishop instructed that the body be left undisturbed and the matter be kept silent. The worker complied with the instructions. However, he has never forgotten the incident and personally believes he had viewed the body of a saint. He had read somewhere that the bodies of true saints are often preserved after death.

GHOST OF CATHERINE SNOW

The complete story of Catherine Snow can be found in
The Hangman is Never Late

During the eighteenth and nineteenth centuries reports of supernatural happenings and ghost sightings often made the pages of local newspapers. It wasn't at all unusual to hear and read of such occurrences soon after an execution. Following the hanging of Catherine Snow from the gallows outside the old court house window located off Duckworth Street, claims spread throughout St. John's of sightings of her spirit. These reported apparitions were even discussed in the newspapers of the day.

Catherine Snow had been found guilty for her part in the murder of her husband, John Snow at Port de Grave. She was sentenced to be hanged, but the execution was delayed six months, after authorities learned she was pregnant. Soon after the birth of her child the execution date was set, and Catherine Snow was executed on Monday, July 21, 1834.

There was a great sense of injustice surrounding this case, and many people felt an innocent woman had gone to the gallows. The body of John Snow had never been found. Catherine had been arrested along with two others; Tobias Mandeville and Arthur Springer, with whom Catherine was having an affair. At the conclusion of the trial the Attorney General told the Court that there was no direct evidence of Catherine Snow's guilt but only a chain of circumstantial evidence.

Even more peculiar was the judge's statement that, "You will observe that nothing said by any of the prisoners can be admitted to implicate her in the act. However, her affair of passion with her very much younger cousin was enough to condemn her." Efforts by the Roman Catholic clergy requesting a commutation of sentence failed.

The night prior to her execution she accepted a glass of wine from Bishop Fleming. When asked why she refused to eat she answered, "Oh what is nourishment to me? God calls upon me to suffer death. That I cannot avoid. But let me add as much as possible to my sufferings so that I may try to make that death worthwhile."

Before the executioner placed the rope around her neck she said, "I was a wretched woman but as innocent of any participation in the crime of murder as an unborn child." At that period in history the Roman Catholic Church would not approve of an executed person being buried in consecrated ground. However, the clergy in this case felt the victim was innocent and she was given a Christian burial, and laid to rest in the Catholic Cemetery. At that time the RC cemetery was located at the foot of Long's Hill in the area now occupied by the Kirk.

Many claims were made of sightings of the ghost of Catherine Snow in the area of the old courthouse and the RC cemetery. These stories were long forgotten by the turn of the century. I remember telling the students of Holy Cross School the tragic story of Catherine Snow during a Book Week appearance there. One student asked me if the remains of Catherine Snow were still buried beneath the Kirk. I answered to the amusement of those present, "I think so. The last place almighty God is going to look for a Catholic is beneath the Kirk."

FORAN'S HOTEL

Originally appeared in Strange but True Newfoundland Stories

One of the many ghost stories told in old time St. John's involves Foran's Hotel, which was located on the site now occupied by the Sir Humphrey Gilbert Building on Duckworth Street.

The belief that the hotel was haunted was so widespread that city folk shunned it for more than a month.

Foran's (The Atlantic) Hotel

The ghastly happenings started on one cold winter night when guests were awakened by a loud knocking. The noise startled them and they gathered in the hallways puzzling over what was taking place. Two men left the group to conduct a search of the hotel to try and solve the mystery. They traced the sound to an upstairs room. Upon entering, the noise suddenly stopped. The men searched the room high and low but could find nothing to explain the occurrence.

Each night after the guests had settled down for the night the knocking would resume and always end when someone entered the vacant room. Word of the haunting noises spread throughout the city and people began staying away from the hotel. Eventually the haunting faded out and customers began to return. Six months later a stranger registered. He was escorted to the haunted room by a staff member who found humour in the fact that they finally had a guest for the room. Adding to the stranger's visit was speculation among hotel staff and guests that the stranger was a hangman from Canada.

At midnight a sudden thunderous knocking erupted and people rushed to the hallways. The noise was much louder than ever before and brought the hotel owner/manager to the scene. He went to the room and after calling to the occupant and not receiving a reply he unlocked and open the door. The pounding stopped. But lying on the floor was the hangman, with a terrified expression on his face.

When the undertaker went into the room to remove the body the knocking broke out again, and lasted about a minute. The stranger was buried at the General Protestant Cemetery on Waterford Bridge Road ... and the knocking in the hotel stopped forever. John Foran, was a prominent member of the Royal St. John's Regatta Committee and owned the boat the Placentia Crew used to win the 1877 Fishermen's Race at Quidi Vidi. He was often called upon to tell the story of the ghost at Foran's Hotel.

AN ORIENTAL PALACE AT QUIDI VIDI LAKE

A splendid structure was once built at the head of Quidi Vidi Lake by the eccentric Professor Charles Danielle. It opened on Regatta Day of 1893. The palace which was named the Royal Lake Pavilion was described in an advertisement in the *Evening Telegram* prior to the 1894 Regatta. It read:

> The above magnificent Oriental Palace will be open to the genteel and respectable public on Regatta Day and every day where everything obtainable at the best hotels on this side of the Atlantic will be served by young lady and gentlemen attendants.
>
> The attendants will be attired in Oriental costumes, and in harmony with the general surroundings — the whole presenting a scene of grandeur that none but Danielles has ever yet gladdened the eyes of Newfoundland with.
>
> The lower, or Banquet Hall, will be for the exclusive catering of dainty refreshments while the Ball Room will be used exclusively as a dining room where hot dinners will be served from 11:30 to 3 p.m. at one dollar each, and teas from 4 p.m. to 8 p.m. at sixty cents.
>
> Four ranges will be operated so that all dinners will be served hot (RED HOT) while an army of table waiters, servants and attendants for every department will assure quick service.
>
> No malts or spirits will be sold in the Pavilion, nor have I any interest in any other tent or booth on the grounds; If I had a regular license, I would lay its privileges aside on Regatta Day. The Pavilion is large, light , airy, cool, high toned, respectable, grand in every respect and detail....and still Joseph doesn't like it.

The Oriental Palace, after it was relocated to Octagon Pond, and re-named the Octagon Castle.

The Palace could accommodate 1500 people in its ball room..

The eccentric Professor tore down the Pavilion in 1895

after being harassed by the man from whom he leased the land. Danielle claimed the landlord wanted him off the land because he was in competition with the landlord who also operated a restaurant/inn. No doubt the landlord was the Joseph referred to in the newspaper ad. The Professor accused the landlord of acts of vandalism against his property and assaults upon his staff.

The Professor carted the wood from the torn down Palace to the Railway Station at Fort William (now Hotel Newfoundland) and had it transported by train to the Octagon Pond where he built his famous Octagon Castle.

Professor Danielle was as eccentric and flamboyant in death as he was in life. A grave in the Anglican Cemetery marks his final resting place. It also contains what the *Evening Telegram* described in 1902 as, "The most elaborate casket that was ever seen in these parts." Not only did

The coffin which Professou Danielle made and which he kept on public display at the Octagon Castle.

32

the Professor design and build his own casket; he also placed it on public display in his Octagon Castle/Restaurant and Inn.

The resplendent walnut casket was covered with black satin and embroidered with gold. The Professor patiently made over eight thousand white satin shells which he used to upholster the interior and an embroidered Orphean Lyre decorated the side. The casket had a glass lid. On display inside were the white satin shroud and golden slippers in which he was eventually buried. The Professor died and was buried during May, 1902. His funeral attracted one of the largest spectator turnouts St. John's had ever witnessed. The spectacular casket was placed in a marble vault. The years have taken their toll on the horizontal monument marking the grave site but the name of Professor Charles Danielle and other information is still easily read.

The Professor's grave is adjacent to the grave of Tasker Cook, a former Mayor of the City of St. John's, and is located along the pathway starting from the entrance on the Forest Road side of the Anglican Cemetery.

THE FIGHTING GHOSTS OF MILITARY ROAD

A ghost story told often around St. John's at the turn of the twentieth century was based on a true incident which took place just east of the Roman Catholic Basilica on Military Road. Many people claimed to have witnessed a man being beaten by another man, but when they approached the two figures they completely disappeared.

The story was no doubt inspired by a murder which took place at the site on December 27, 1848 on Military

Road. The body of Kevin Wilson was found on Military Road, covered in blood, on the morning of December 27, 1848. Wilson had been killed by a blow to the head with a heavy object. Police were unable to solve the crime and it remained a mystery for almost a year.

Then a strange occurrence at sea solved the mystery for police.

During August 1849, the brigantine *Star* set sail from St. John's with a new crewmember on board named Isaac O'Neill. As the ship sailed along the coast, the captain noticed O'Neill's strange behaviour. He was depressed, avoided others and had lost his appetite. When questioned by Captain William Bennett, O'Neill began sobbing and admitted to murdering Wilson with a club the previous year.

Even though he was comforted by the Captain, the murder of Wilson continued to weigh heavily on his mind. While on watch the following night, he jumped overboard. Captain Bennett immediately launched a life boat but O'Neill swam away from it. He turned, waved to his would-be rescuers and disappeared beneath the deep waters.

GOWER STREET GHOSTS

An account of the supernatural which made headlines in the St. John's newspapers took place about 1907 on Gower Street, and upset the neighbourhood for weeks thereafter.

The uncanny story began when a Newfoundland couple living in the United States returned to St. John's to live. They rented a house on Gower Street near the Victoria Street intersection and paid three months rent in advance.

They ended up spending only one night in the house.

Subsequently, stories of strange happenings in the house spread rapidly and reached the offices of the *Evening Telegram*. When a *Telegram* reporter met with the horrified couple he was told that, "...the woman had been startled in the night by a series of blood-curdling screeches. Horrified she sat up in bed and saw a woman who had been known to her, but had died several years earlier — in the same room."

Adding to the horror, according to the *Telegram* story, "The apparition was dragging another woman — who was also known to be dead — by the hair of her head. The woman being dragged was screaming." The housewife passed out and was not revived until daybreak. The couple took their personal belongings and left the house immediately, never to return. The newspaper also noted, "...the landlord refused to refund the rent."

The couple moved to a flat on Goodview Street and neighbours there recalled later that the woman who saw the screaming spirits never got over her experience.

Meanwhile, in a three-storey Victorian style house on Gower Street near Hotel Newfoundland, unusual occurrences were reported during the late 1970s. After several families had fled the house, never to return, neighbours began calling Open Line host Ron Pumphrey to report the phenomena. The stories included the sounds of a sobbing child coming from the attic late at night; the rattling of chains; the sound of footsteps from the attic; and blood-curdling screams.

The stories continued for some weeks and the landlord found it impossible to rent the vacant home.

After things settled down, a priest was called in to bless each room in the home. Soon after it was sold, and in time the stories of hauntings faded from the public mind.

THE FIERY GHOST OF BAY BULLS ROAD

Another strange and ghastly phenomenon took place in a house on Bay Bulls Road during 1910. A trouting party from St. John's became stranded in that area when a sudden wind and rainstorm struck. They found refuge in a vacant house and although they had concerns about it, they decided to wait out the storm until morning.

At midnight they were horrified by the manifestation of fire. The men watched in terror as the flaming figure of a man threw himself against the front of the house; passed through the walls and out the other side.

The manifestation was described as, "...red-hot, glowing, aggressive and was accompanied by a hurricane gust of wind." When the wind died down the phantom disappeared. The men recalled that during the apparition the house shook. But no visible sign of the phantom was left.

THE HAUNTING AT HIGGIN'S LINE

Bute's Fortress was a notable nineteenth century structure located near Long Pond in an area once known as the Sand Pits. It derived its name from the owner, Captain Bute, an officer of the English Garrison in St. John's.

The home was constructed to resemble a fortress and even had its own dungeon. Known for his cruelty, Bute frequently used it to discipline soldiers and servants.

An uncanny event occurred several nights after Bute imprisoned a servant in the dungeon. In the midst of a large party at the fortress a terrible commotion interrupted the event. The sounds came from the dungeon. The terrified Bute recalled the helpless servant locked up below the fortress. With weapons drawn Bute followed by several others rushed below to the dungeon. What they found startled them and caused guests to flee the building.

The servant lay dead in a corner of the dungeon. The expression on his face showed extreme terror and shock. Although Bute examined the area he could find no explanation for either the commotion or the death. City people believed it was retribution heaped upon Bute by the soul of the dead servant.

FLOATING COFFIN
Originally appeared in Jack Fitzgerald's Notebook

During the early part of the nineteenth century, people in the area of the waterfront claimed to have seen a ghastly, fog-like apparition of a coffin moving across the St. John's Harbour at night.

Captain Patrick Spry, who often told the story to his children, believed it was told to keep young children away from the wharves after dark. Spry claimed the casket was supposed to carry the body of a seaman murdered on the waterfront in the eighteenth century. Like so many other ghost stories over the centuries, this one faded from public memory. However, it appears to have had its origins in the true tale of one of the most unusual funerals ever to take place in Newfoundland.

The ghastly funeral took place on St. John's Harbour on October 28, 1794. The silence of that morning was broken by the steady and morbid beating of military drums along the shoreline as a flotilla of dories, one of them carrying a flag draped coffin, moved slowly over the harbour waters. On shore, standing at attention in honour of the deceased, were three companies of Newfoundland volunteer servicemen, the entire crews of six British men-of-war, and crowds of city residents.

This uncanny funeral was being held to honour the slain Lieutenant Richard Lawry who had been murdered several days before during an ambush by a group of St. John's Irish immigrants. The Lieutenant was an officer on the HMS *Boston*, and he had angered the locals by impressing* a group of their friends into service on the *Boston*. They waited on shore near Waldegrave Street and when Lawry came ashore they ambushed and beat him to death.

The Governor felt that a trial and execution of the guilty was absolutely necessary to preserve order throughout the island. One of the ambushers accepted the Governor's offer of immunity in return for identifying the killers. Almost immediately Richard Power and Garrett Farrell were arrested and charged with murder. The trial and execution were swift.

They were tried on Wednesday, sentenced on Thursday and executed on Friday. The hangings took place near Fort Townshend. Their bodies were then turned over to local surgeons for dissection, which was part of the sentence for murder.

Before departing for England the Governor offered a reward of £50 for information leading to the arrest of a third man involved in the murder — William Barrows. However, Barrows is believed to have fled Newfoundland, and was never found.

Meanwhile, the victim, Lieutenant Lawry, was laid to rest at the old Anglican cemetery opposite the present

---

* In those days British naval officers frequently led press gangs, which conscripted able bodied men into the British navy, usually against their will, to replace those sailors who had become sick or injured.

Courthouse on Duckworth Street. Captain Spry said those who claim to have seen the floating coffin on the harbour believed it was the ghost of Lawry.

THE MIRACLE PHOTOGRAPH

For three days in May during 1947, hundreds of people in St. John's visited the intersection of Bate's Hill and Henry Street to view what the press had described as the "Miracle of Argentia." On display in the window of Marshall's Studio at that location was an amazing picture which had attracted international attention. This rare photo was astonishing for what appeared in the picture as well as what did not appear.

The 'Miracle Picture Story' had its beginning in a family home at Freshwater, Placentia Bay. The Wakeham family had moved from Petite Forte to Placentia during January, 1947. Eleven year old Ignatius Wakeham, an altar boy at the Roman Catholic Parish Church at Freshwater, was ecstatic when his older brother gave him a slide. Sliding down snow-covered hills was one of the most popular forms of winter recreation during that era.

What started as a fun afternoon for young Ignatius ended in tragedy and deep sorrow throughout the Placentia area. While sliding down a hill Ignatius was run over by a taxi and killed.

In accordance with tradition at that time, the boy was waked in his home at Freshwater.

On the day of his funeral his mother wanted a last picture taken of the boy. She asked three of his altar boy friends to stand alongside the coffin for the picture. An old box camera was used to take the photograph. Then the coffin lid was closed and the funeral took place.

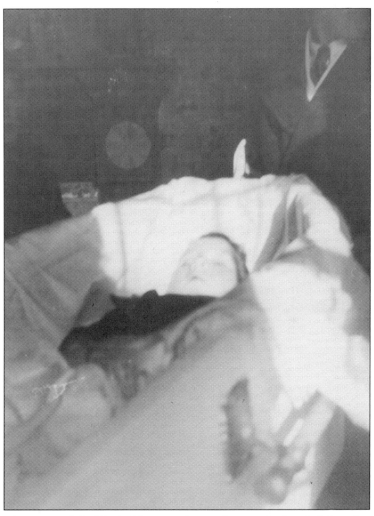

The image of the Virgin Mary can be seen here at the head of the coffin, clearly visible against the dark background.

About a week later when Mrs. Wakeham picked up the photos she was startled by the picture taken of young Ignatius and the altar boys. Mysteriously, not one of the three altar boys appeared in the picture. In their place was a small statue-like figure of the Blessed Virgin Mary, looking down at young Ignatius and holding out what appeared to be a flower in her hand.

The Wakeham's asked the photo shop to look through the pictures and see if double exposure had taken place. It had not. During subsequent weeks the story of the miracle picture spread by word of mouth throughout the area. Mrs. Wakeham kindly allowed curious visitors into her home to view the picture. In May, almost four months later, word of the Miracle Picture reached St. John's and the *Sunday Herald* immediately dispatched two reporters and a photographer to Freshwater to investigate the story and hopefully get a copy of the picture.

They arrived at the Wakeham home after nightfall and were warmly welcomed. Mrs. Wakeham showed them the picture and retold the story — which she had told so often over previous months — of circumstances surrounding the taking of the picture. While she did not want the picture published, she did agree to the reporters request to borrow it for several hours to bring it to St. John's and have one special enlargement of the picture made. Mrs. Wakeham also agreed to allow the photograph to be placed on public display in St. John's for its spiritual value to those witnessing it. Later that week the *Sunday Herald* ran banner front page headlines of the size associated with great events like the ending of a war or the death of a Monarch. The headlines read "Miracle At Argentia."

American authorities at the U.S. base at Argentia had already expressed an interest in the picture. They obtained the picture from the family and had base photographic experts study it. Using a special scope they were able to describe in more detail what was in the picture. The features of the Virgin Mary's face were clear and what appeared at first glance at the picture to be flowers in Our

Lady's hands were actual thorn bushes. The experts concluded the photo was authentic. According to the *Herald* several high ranking officers at the American Base described the picture as, "One of the most outstanding things they had ever seen."

In response to photo experts in New York, three enlarged copies of the Miracle Picture were sent there to be examined. This study concluded the picture was authentic and the experts could offer no explanation for what had happened. There was no evidence of it being a double exposure, no evidence of any sort of flaw, and no indication of light reflection.

All the pictures taken with the camera with the same roll of film were examined and experts found no signs of anything unusual. The picture was accepted in Newfoundland as a miracle and treasured by the young boy's mother who found great comfort in the Miracle Picture.

The Wakeham family returned to live at Petite Forte several months after the death of Ignatius.

THE CROSS IN THE SKY

During August of the same year of the Miracle Picture another phenomena took place. On a hot humid August night, many families in the Mundy Pond area were outdoors or sitting on their steps to cool off. Suddenly, the attention of many people was drawn to the skies over the land now occupied by a Housing Development in the Froude Avenue area. A large burning cross could be seen hovering in the night sky.

Among those on Blackmarsh Road who witnessed the burning cross was Angus Dunn. He said, "It was so real you could almost reach out and touch it." The apparition lasted for about thirty minutes and then disappeared. After a brief sensation throughout the City over subsequent weeks it also disappeared from St. John's History — until now.

VICTIMS SPIRITS RETURN

During the 1980s I was approached by tenants of a house on Carter's Hill who claimed the house was being haunted. The person told me that a series of strange and blood-curdling happenings had taken place during the several months he had been renting the house with two other friends. It began with the unexplained sounds of someone walking in the upstairs, and doors opening and closing.

To rule out the possibility of the noises being caused by wind flowing through the open windows the man closed all the windows one night and made sure the several upstairs doors were properly closed.

Several hours later the ritual of walking and opening and closing doors resumed. The man said this was preceded by a cold feeling experienced by all three tenants. On several occasions when the house was left vacant with the door unlocked for short periods of time, they would return to find the doors locked. A back door which could only be locked from the inside and which had been deliberately left unlocked on several occasions was locked when the tenants returned. There was no explanation.

All three tenants said they had felt a cold angry presence in the house at times when strange things were happening. The final straw for them came during Christmas, when the Christmas tree began to shake on its own. Soon after that the men moved out. They were not, however, the only ones to witness these poltergeist type happenings. Neighbours informed me that a family had moved out of the same house a year before after complaining that the house was haunted.

The former tenants feel the hauntings resulted from a triple murder that took place on the street in 1922. The story of these murders is told in *The Hangman is Never Late*. Today Carter's Hill runs from Livingstone Street to LeMarchant Road, however in 1922 the section from Cabot Street to LeMarchant Road was called Murray Street. It was in a house on this street that the triple murder took place. The crime was the most cold blooded murder to happen in Newfoundland since 1872, when Patrick Geehan murdered his wife and brother-in-law.

The killings took place in the Jim Lee Laundry, which was owned and occupied by the three victims. A dispute over wages and working conditions, and the suggestion of family hostilities carried over from China, led to the murders. Wo Fen Game, an employee at the laundry, was angered because one of the owners, Hong Loen, was threatening to fire him and throw him onto the streets. Game could not speak English and viewed this action as a death sentence. He was convinced no one else would hire him, and other Chinese businessmen would ostracize him rather than offend the Jim Lee owners, who had paid to bring Game into Newfoundland.

While this dispute was building Hong Loen told Game that he (Game) would die sooner or later, and that Hong Wing of the Hop Wah laundry intended to kill him. Wing, according to Loen, was determined to kill Game because of a dispute between the two families which had been ongoing back in China for decades.

Game sought the help of his friend Charlie Fong, operator of a Water Street Restaurant. Fong met with Hong Loen in an unsuccessful attempt to conciliate the dispute. When Game learned he had been fired he went to the Royal Stores on Water Street, purchased a gun, and that evening shot and killed the three owners of the Jim Lee Laundry. He then went to the Hop Wah Laundry on Casey Street and shot Hong Wing. Fortunately, Wing was not seriously wounded. Game then walked to the top of Barron Street, raised the gun to his own head and with his hand trembling fired. He was taken to the General Hospital. Upon recovery he was arrested and tried for murder. During the trial he was gagged and tied and held at the back of the Courtroom because his loud moaning was interrupting the proceedings.

While at Her Majesty's Penitentiary he somehow got hold of a gun, and made an unsuccessful attempt to escape. At 8 a.m. on December 16, 1922 Wo Fen Game was escorted to the gallows in the prison yard. When he saw the six foot tall executioner approach him dressed in an overcoat with a woolen hat partially covering his face, his whole body began to tremble. The execution was swift, and the prisoner died at 8:09.

FRIGHTENED BY GHOST
Originally appeared in *Jack Fitzgerald's Notebook*

The diary of Aaron Thomas, preserved at the Newfoundland archives, describes the area between Flower Hill (later changed to Springdale Street) and Flower Hill Street (later changed to Flower Hill) as being the most beautiful natural flower garden in the world. A large field in the area was used as a race track during the early nineteenth century, and the local gentry spent many an enjoyable evening there. It was also the site haunted for a decade by the spirit of Alice Janes, who was among the city's most ardent racing enthusiasts. With her Irish-knit shawl and jug of brew, Alice was a fixture at the race track.

During one of the races there, Alice suffered a heart attack and died instantly. The whole town turned out for the funeral, and she was given a respectable send-off at the old cemetery adjoining the Anglican Cathedral.

A year passed. On the anniversary of Alice's death a young woman was being escorted through the Flower Hill field by a male companion. Darkness was just beginning to set in and the girl complained of a strange, cold feeling. She asked her friend to take her home. As they neared the edge of the field they came upon a sight that sent them screaming from the field. They later described the apparition to friends. At first it seemed like an old woman sitting on a rock holding a jug in her hand. When the couple neared the figure, it slowly stood up and stared straight at them. Her eyes were burning red and her white hair stood out like the whisks of a broom.

The couple swore it was the ghost of Alice Janes. When word of the apparition spread throughout town, several friends of the late Alice Janes visited the field and then the gravesite to pray. While at the grave side they noticed that the wooden Celtic cross marker that they had placed in the ground to indicate the grave had disappeared. They searched the area but failed to find it.

A later newspaper account noted that the apparition of Alice haunted the Flower Hill field for a decade after. Then one day the caretaker at the cemetery, while clearing an area of the old graveyard, found the missing cross. He placed it back on the gravesite. There were no more sightings of the apparition, and old-timers believed that her spirit had finally found peace.

THE HILL O'CHIPS BANSHEE

Originally appeared in *Strange but True Newfoundland Stories*

Stories of banshees are common in Irish folklore, but surprisingly, and considering our strong Irish roots, they are practically unheard of in Newfoundland culture. However, we do have an interesting banshee story which attracted public attention in St. John's during the late eighteenth century. The story involved some strange events leading up to the death of a prominent St. John's man and widespread claims among inhabitants that he had been taken by the banshee.

Most families in the city during that period had some strange tradition or unusual token associated with their family history. The family of St. John's businessman William Welsh immigrated from Ireland, bringing with them the family curse of the Banshee. Welsh himself gave little credence to the curse, but his wife and three sons did. Welsh was a healthy robust fellow, who operated a public house and banquet hall on the west side of the Hill o' Chips. His wife was an accomplished cook and their banquet hall was famous.

One night, Mrs. Welsh became terror-stricken when she heard the cry of the banshee at her window. By the time she alerted her husband it had disappeared. Describing the banshee cry, Mrs. Welsh told her husband, "It was like a weirdly wailing and sobbing Keyne (professional Irish mourner), coming nearer and nearer each moment until it reached the window. Then with a wild shriek it died away with unearthly sobbing. Anyone hearing it would never forget it."

The next day the Welsh's youngest son Felix cut an artery while chopping fire wood and almost died. Still, William would not acknowledge belief in the banshee.

Some years passed and on the occasion of his sixtieth birthday he found himself sitting at the head table in his banquet hall. He was accompanied by the most prominent citizens of St. John's, who had come to help him celebrate.

Suddenly, the door swung open. Framed in the doorway, with a deathly pale face, stood William's eldest son Michael. He was oblivious to all else except his father — at whom he stared. A sudden silence fell as he made his way towards his father. "We all heard the cry tonight," he said. "Are you all right." William, somewhat surprised, answered, "Of course I am. Why wouldn't I be? I'm as healthy as an ox."

When Michael left the room, Colonel Skinner of the regiment in St. John's asked William what Michael meant when he referred to "the cry." William then told the attentive audience the story of the banshee. He said that, "The Welsh's since time immemorial were from the chiefs of a barony in Ireland, and from the first Welsh, a great chief and warrior, the banshee's cry always foretold either a death or some ill fortune of one of them."

He added that although it was only tradition his wife and sons firmly believed in it. When he concluded this story many in the room agreed with the family. Colonel Skinner, however, was a little doubtful. But he expressed the opinion it was certainly a colourful piece of folklore. When the guests left, Welsh scolded his wife and children for allowing a silly superstition to bother them. He said, "No one should concern himself about me; I never felt better in my life." The family then retired for the night.

The following morning at breakfast, without any warning or indication that something was wrong, Welsh died. When Colonel Skinner heard the news he was shocked. "I can't believe it. He was so healthy." he said. But then, recalling Welsh's tale of the banshee, he added, "There was something in the banshee's cry after all."

FEILDIAN GROUNDS HAUNTING

During the mid-nineteenth century St. John's abounded with claims that the spirit of a soldier on horseback haunted the bridge at Pringledale. Pringledale was a meadow area which is now occupied by Feildian Grounds, Pringle Place and part of Rennies Mill Road. The claim was that residents returning to town at night after a day in the country saw the spirit of a man murdered at Pringledale, near Rennies River Bridge. The ghostly apparition was of a man in military uniform with blood pouring from a wound in his chest, mounted on a black stallion.

Stories of this nature were common for the time. However, they usually were inspired by a true event and told and re-told until they became part of the city's colourful folklore. The Ghost of Pringledale had its origins in a true life drama which unfolded in 1826 at the location, and resulted in the death of a British soldier from Fort Townshend. That story is told in more detail in my book *The Hangman is Never Late.*

On March 30, 1826 a duel to the death was fought at Pringledale between two soldiers from the garrison at Fort Townshend. Captain Mark Rudkin, a twenty-two year veteran of the Royal Newfoundland Veteran Company and Ensign J. Philpot, known for his mean disposition, became involved in a dispute over a card game the night before at Fort Townshend.

Ensign Philpot insulted Rudkin and kicked him in the rear end as the Captain left the game in disgust over the Ensign's behaviour. Humiliated by young Philpot, Captain Rudkin demanded an apology, or else satisfaction would be sought in the gentlemen's way, meaning a duel. Philpot refused to apologize and on March 30 the duel at Pringledale took place.

Noted city historian, Dr. Paul O'Neill, noted in his writings that it was said that Philpot's horse shied three times before crossing the bridge at Rennie's River on the morning of the duel. Perhaps an omen of what was to happen that day.

Captain Rudkin, an expert marksman, sought only to frighten Philpot and teach him a lesson. He got off the first shot but deliberately missed his target. Philpot also missed his target but not deliberately. His intention to fight to the death was obvious by his behaviour at the duel. Prior to the duel the ensign removed his flannel waistcoat and shirt to reduce chances of the flannel entering any wounds he might receive. He wore only a linen shirt and trousers while Captain Rudkin was dressed in full military uniform.

Rudkin was prepared to stop the duel after the first round if the young Ensign would apologize. However, Philpot flatly refused and a second round of duelling took place. This time both guns fired simultaneously, but Philpot completely missed his target. Rudkin did not. He placed a bullet straight into the heart of Ensign Philpot who died instantly.

Although Rudkin was tried for murder, he was acquitted. Members of the jury included Tom Brookings, one of the founders of the Royal St. John's Regatta, and Benjamin Bowring, founder of Bowring Brothers Ltd.

MIRACLE ON SIGNAL HILL
Originally appeared in *Strange but True Newfoundland Stories*

An unexplained incident — involving the noon-day gun at Signal Hill, St. John's — which happened during 1890, left city people believing a miracle had taken place. A diphtheria epidemic had raged throughout the city that year, and had spread to Portugal Cove. Among its victims were Canon Smith, the parson there, and his four children.

Through the efforts of Judge D.W. Prowse and Dr. Fraser, the Smiths were taken to the old hospital on Signal Hill (this hospital was destroyed in the fire of 1892). Three of the Smith children had died and nine-year-old Harold was suffering through his last days on earth.

Parson Smith wrote in his diary of little Harold's final day. He noted,

> A strong breeze of wind was blowing on the day that Harold died. He was a bright lad, but his nerves were highly strung and he was easily excited. While at 10:30 a.m. I watched him as he was lying quietly in his bed, the wind slammed one of the doors of the hospital.
>
> The noise so affected little Harold that his face became for a few moments distorted by pain and turned quite purple. After some considerable time he became easier. Glancing at my watch, I saw it was only four minutes to 12 noon, and then I thought of the noon gun which was planted above the hospital, right on the hill back of it.
>
> The report from that gun I knew would soon thunder over the hospital shaking the whole building. I was in an agony of mind as to what would happen then to little Harold.

Canon Smith was haunted by an incident many years before in which a young girl, viewing the motionless body of her dying father screamed so loudly that he sat up in bed

51

and lingered for nearly two hours in horrible agony, before death came to relieve his suffering.

Smith continued with his account of his son's last day:

> I was beside myself with fear of what I believed would soon be enacted in the room where my boy and I were. Then a voice spoke to my inmost soul: "seek," it said, "and ye shall receive."
>
> I can't remember exactly what I said in the agony of prayer on that occasion, but I think it was something like this, "O Lord, who did shut the mouth of lions, of thy pity muzzle that gun."
>
> I thought that the great God would give his angels charge to shield my little lad so that he would not be disturbed by the report of the gun.

Parson Smith watched the time until one o'clock but the gun did not fire. He said, "I knew that God had answered my prayer. At 1:30 little Henry slipped peacefully into eternity."

A Mr. Scott was in charge of the noon-day gun at the time, and he couldn't explain why the gun did not fire that day. He said, "Three times I put a new primer into her and pulled the lanyard, but the old girl wouldn't speak. It was all no use. I feared to prime her again lest some fire might be in the vent and fire the gun while I was in the act of priming it. The next day I tried her again and she answered at once to the first pull of the lanyard."

When Parson Smith recovered he told his congregation at Portugal Cove about God's little miracle on Signal Hill.

THE GHOST IN THE EMPTY APARTMENT

During the late 1970s a family moved out of a New Gower Street apartment because they were convinced the house was haunted. Their concerns were reinforced after they spoke with previous tenants who also complained of weird, unexplained happenings experienced in the same apartment.

The apartment was located above a small convenience store on the north side of New Gower Street, near the Pleasant Street intersection. The uncanny happenings however, were not occurring in the occupied house but from rooms adjacent in the building next door, which housed only a grocery store and a vacant upstairs apartment.

The lady who approached me on the story claimed that soon after moving into the house she began to hear noises from the room adjacent to her kitchen in the adjoining building. At first she thought someone had left a radio operating. This happened intermittently, and on one occasion her babysitter complained to her that the people next door were arguing loudly. Over subsequent weeks, the lady turned off her own radio and television and listened. Usually, after 11 p.m. she would hear the sounds of muffled voices and doors opening and closing and someone walking up and down the stairs.

One day she approached the owner of the next door building and asked who was living in the upstairs apartment. She was astonished when he told her, "Nobody. I have never rented that as an apartment." She then told him of the nightly noises. The owner was concerned and his first thoughts were that teens in the neighbourhood were breaking in and using the place so he made a search, accompanied by the tenant from next door. They could find no indication that the place was being used, or any signs of a forced entry. All windows were appropriately locked from the inside, and the front and back doors were locked each evening when the store closed.

There was one room that had a padlock on it, and it turned out to be the room the lady was complaining about. The store owner then told her a tale which sent shivers up her spine. He said he didn't know the whole story, but people in the neighbourhood had told him that decades before a young girl had been shot to death in that room. Bloodstains dried into the wall were still visible. He didn't know anything more about the story or even if it was true.

When the lady approached me, I did some research on the building and learned that in the late nineteenth century it was a tavern operated by Francis Canning.* In an upstairs room in that building Canning had shot to death his barmaid, Mary Nugent of Kelligrews. Nugent had just told him that she was leaving her job to get married. Canning was very upset by the news and confronted the young girl in the upstairs room at 3 p.m. on May 12, 1899. They argued over her decision and he pulled a revolver and shot and killed her. She did not die right away. She was taken to the General Hospital and Canning, under police escort, was allowed to visit her. Before passing away she forgave him.

Our justice system did not. He was tried, convicted of murder and sentenced to hang. Canning told guards at Her Majesty's Penitentiary, "I will never flinch when going to the scaffold." His execution took place on July 29, 1899. The night before the execution he sat and chatted with his wife, two children and his sister-in-law in his cell. They left

---

* The story of Francis Canning is told in more detail in my book *The Hangman is Never Late*.

the prison at 10:30 p.m. and at 11 p.m. he had a snack of tea and toast.

One of the worst thunder and lightning storms to strike the city in nearly fifty years was raging outside as the prison bell began to toll at 7:45 a.m. Canning walked firmly to the gallows, fulfilling his promise not to flinch. His last words were "Lord have mercy on my soul. Into thy hands O Lord, I commend my spirit. Lord have mercy on my soul." Canning was cut down and after doctors confirmed death had taken place he was buried about thirty feet from the gallows.

Canning lived in a three-storey house on Theatre Hill (now Queen's Road). The house is still there today and located east of City Hall on the north side of the street. I have talked to several families who lived in that house over the past century and none had any unusual, strange or ghostly stories to tell.

GOULDS GHOST
Originally appeared in Jack Fitzgerald's Notebook

Shoal Harbour is only minutes south of the Goulds in the west end of St. John's. It is the site of an alleged buried treasure and hauntings. The famous Diver Dobbin of St. Mary's Bay was a man of great courage, and even during the 1870s when he himself witnessed a strange apparition while digging for pirate's gold at Shoal Harbour, he was not deterred.

The story of buried treasure at Shoal Harbour was a well known story even in those days and Dobbin, the veteran of many such adventures, teamed up with eight men from St. John's on a treasure hunting expedition to retrieve the gold. When they arrived at the site which the map indicated held the gold, it was too dark to start work. While discussing plans to dig for the treasure, Dobbin recalled, they were all seized with an uncanny feeling and an unidentifiable dread. To break the spell, Dobbin grabbed a pick and started to dig. After a few minutes Captain Martin screamed and fell to the ground. When he regained consciousness, the men asked him what had frightened him and he refused to answer.

Dobbin led the men back to a nearby house where they were staying. Captain Martin went straight to bed while the others remained in the kitchen making light of the Martin incident. Suddenly, a loud knock was heard at the door, which was fastened by a wooden button inside. Before anyone could open the door, it flew open and a man came to the centre of the kitchen. He stood motionless on the floor and made no sound. The move was so frightening that everyone in the room except Dobbin and Moran passed out. Dobbin noted that he too was frightened but he kept calm.

Then in front of the phantom figure there appeared the bodies of eight men lying motionless on the floor. Dobbin described the phantom as middle height and stoutly built. He wore a cap underneath which could be seen a mass of short black curls. He wore dark cloth pants, a blue coat, cut sailor fashion square across the hips. He disappeared as suddenly as he came.

When Breen, one of the men who had fainted, regained consiousness his foot, which was close to the open flame, was on fire. One of the men grabbed a knife and moved towards him to cut the clothing away. Another member of the party had just come into the room and thought the man was trying to kill Breen so he tried to wrestle the knife away. Diver Dobbin intervened, took the knife away and put out the fire on Breen's clothing. The figures of the eight men on the floor vanished.

The treasure hunt came to an end when Captain Martin told Dobbin and the others that the ghost in the kitchen was the same ghost he had seen at the treasure site. The men pledged to leave the area and never return. The last words Captain Martin said to Dobbin were, "The gold will have to lay there till the Day of Judgement."

THE GHOST OF MOUNT CARMEL CEMETERY

During the last year of World War Two, a young St. John's woman dropped dead suddenly walking up Barter's Hill, towards her home on Monroe Street. The woman had been downtown shopping for a suitable gift for her brother, who was returning from the war in Europe that week on board a Canadian naval ship. It was Monday, and the ship was due on Saturday.

As was the practice she was waked for two nights in her home and the burial scheduled for Wednesday. Her parents persuaded church authorities to allow her remains to be stored in the chapel at Mount Carmel Cemetery until Friday so her brother could pay his last respects. The deceased had been a member of the Presentation Convent Girls Choir and loved the hymn, Ave Maria. Her love for the Ave Maria was mentioned many times by her friends during the wake.

On Saturday her brother arrived in St. John's, and was taken by family in an OK Taxi to Mount Carmel Cemetery. The taxi moved slowly up the very narrow driveway leading to the chapel area, and the driver pulled into the side. As the family exited the taxi they could hear an organist playing the Ave Maria. The music had a very soothing affect on everyone, and it was believed by the family that the parish priest had arranged the music as part of the final funeral ceremony before the deceased was laid to rest.

However, when they arrived at the door of the chapel it was locked. The father felt it may have jammed and tried at first to push it open but without success. Meanwhile, the organist continued to play the Ave Maria. Then the caretaker and priest arrived and unlocked the door. The chapel was empty except for the casket of the deceased girl. Everyone present was bewildered by what had happened and nobody could explain it.

The girl's brother, who passed away in the 1980s, believed to the day he died that the unexplained organ music was something inspired by his dead sister to let him know she was happy and at peace.

DINTY MEETS LUCIFER

Caul's Field was a large meadow between Brazil Street and Casey Street, and north of Monroe Street. The boys of the Old Centre Town area used it as their own recreational facility when Cauls' horses were not grazing. During the early 1950s there was an intriguing supernatural story associated with the field. For decades people in the neighbourhood believed the field was haunted by no less a spirit than Lucifer himself. Several people had died instantly while walking through the field at night. While the official reasons for death was heart attack the neighbourhood had another explanation.

There had been widely-told stories of people seeing a mystical dark figure, believed to be Lucifer, moving around the field at night. The story was frightening enough to keep school-age children from frequenting the area after sundown. But it wasn't credible enough to keep the older neighbourhood boys from hanging out in the field late at night.

One such night the boys from Flower Hill — including Dinty Hearn, Fatso Ryall, Trapper Gillett, Dino Caul, Buff O'Keefe, Dickey Murphy and a few others — after playing a game of baseball stayed around until long after dark telling ghost stories. One which gave the boy's goose pimples was the Lucifer story. As it neared midnight, one by one the boys began leaving the field to go home. However, Dinty had fallen asleep and the boys left him sleeping near an old shed.

Soon after midnight, Dinty awoke and was angry that he had been left alone by his friends. With the Lucifer story foremost in his mind he began to walk out of the field. He was suddenly startled by the sight of a huge black figure blocking his way on the path leading to Brazil Street. He froze! Dinty was one of the gutsiest fellows in town and he wasn't ready to back down even from Lucifer himself.

Dintly picked up a long piece of two by four and when he got near enough to Lucifer he swung the board with all his might striking the mystical figure with great force. He suddenly found himself flying arse of kettle through the air and landed in nearby bushes. When he came to, the dark figure was just a few feet away from him and he was able to see it clearly for the first time. Lucifer, turned out to be Billy Caul's black stallion, Mighty Joe. Mighty Joe had responded to Dinty's assault with a kick of his own. Dinty swore that the story was true. Some ghost stories are like that!

EXORCIST VISITS FLATROCK

In 1954 a supernatural occurrence at Flatrock, just east of St. John's, attracted much public attention and became the centre of a police investigation. The bizarre happening was reported in the media, investigated by the RCMP and the St. John's Fire Department, and in the end remained as mysterious as when it first came to public attention.

The owner of the home, Mike Parsons, told reporters he had hoped that some research group would investigate the supernatural happenings in his home. His wife, Josephine, had become so upset that she became ill and a priest was called in to bless the home. The bizarre story began in November with the sudden appearance of a flame. Mrs. Parsons told reporters, "We were in the kitchen and smelled smoke. In the woodbox we found a dictionary burning. There were boughs and dry sticks there, but they were not burning. We were puzzled, but let it go at that."

Several days later Mrs. Parsons and her daughter were in the kitchen while Mr. Parsons was in the barn milking cows. Josephine recalled, "We smelled smoke and started looking around for fire but couldn't find any. I called out to Dad and Uncle Jim and they came rushing in to look around."

The source of fire was blamed on a sack of sugar located in the corner of the kitchen which had suddenly burst into flames giving off a bad odour. Mr. Parsons puzzled by the event later commented, "Here's the mysterious thing about it. I touched the sugar sack — just touched it with my hand and the fire went out."

When reporters went to investigate reports coming out of Flatrock of strange happenings they were taken on a tour of the house. They were shown a bureau in an upstairs room with a groove burned into it. The damage resulted when a box of holy literature resting on it suddenly burst into flames.

In another incident a doll belonging to a grandchild of the Parsons was resting on the kitchen floor when it suddenly became consumed by fire which seemingly burst out from within the doll. In a separate incident a bedroom with no wires or chimney near it had mysteriously burned in several corners after the sudden eruption of flame. The flame died out on its own.

The mystery sparked a great deal of speculation among the people of Flatrock. The most sceptical suggested it was being deliberately developed so the owners could collect on insurance. However, the RCMP ruled out that possibility noting that no insurance was carried on the property. The Parsons had a summer's harvest of vegetables stored in the cellar, and the adjoining barn housed five sheep, a cow, a calf, a horse and twelve tons of hay. They certainly had no interest in losing their possessions in a fire.

A priest visited the house and performed the rites of exorcism. Meanwhile the results of the RCMP investigation — which were inconclusive — were sent to the Justice Department. The amazing flames of Flatrock have never been explained. Some attributed the unexplained incidents to the work of a poltergeist which is a noisy, mischievous spirit.

PSYCHIC EXPERIENCE

While fire swept through the Knights of Columbus Hostel on Harvey Road on December 14, 1942, more than a hundred miles away Elizabeth Ryan sensed something was wrong. Her two sons, Gabriel and Laurence Ryan, were at the Knights of Columbus Hostel that night when fire destroyed the building and claimed ninety-nine lives.

So real was her sense of danger that she spent most of the night in solemn prayer asking God to protect and keep her sons safe. The next morning neighbours told her of the disaster of the night before at the K of C in St. John's. On the night of the fire, she had been at home listening to the radio broadcast of the Uncle Tim's Barn Dance Show from the K of C. At the time the station went off the air, Mrs. Ryan assumed it had ceased operations due to technical problems.

Unaware of what was happening she turned her radio off and began preparing for bed. Then a strange thing happened. It was at this instant she felt her sons were in danger. Most old-timers describe it as an omen, or psychic warning of pending danger. While walking through the house she felt something brush against her leg. She assumed it was the family cat. For some unknown reason, she suddenly became concerned about her sons.

She searched the house for the cat and realized she had let the cat out earlier. Perplexed by the incident, she was confronted with the unseen force a second time. A feeling of dread gripped her. She said, "I knelt on my knees and prayed. I prayed the whole night."

The following morning the community was alive with reports of the previous night's destruction and loss of life at the K of C. Mrs. Ryan realized then, that the omen she

The Knights of Columbus Hostel fire at the height of the blaze.

had experienced that night was a warning that her sons were in danger.

Throughout that day and part of the next the Ryan family worried and prayed as they awaited news from or about the boys. On the evening of December 14 their prayers were answered when Mrs. Ryan received a telegram from Gabriel and Laurence, stating they were both safe and there was no need to worry.

LADY PEARL'S GHOST

During the latter part of the nineteenth century many people had claimed to have seen the phantom figure of a lady riding a white horse in an area west of St. John's and now part of Mount Pearl. It was believed to be an apparition of Lady Anne Pearl, wife of Sir James Pearl for whom Mount Pearl is named.

Captain Pearl was a British Navy veteran who fought in the Napoleonic Wars and was decorated by the British and Dutch governments.

The Pearls were given a large grant of land near St. John's and retired there in 1829. In 1830 Captain Pearl returned to England to congratulate the new King, William IV, and to present a petition for responsible government for Newfoundland. He was accompanied by Charles Fox Bennett, Thomas Brookings and John Job.

Captain Pearl passed away suddenly at St. John's on January 13, 1840. The Pearl home had burned down the same year he died, and his wife had it rebuilt.

Lady Pearl had been a familiar sight riding her horse on the estate, and, after her death in England in 1860, stories spread throughout St. John's that the grounds were being haunted by her ghost. The sightings were described as Lady Pearl, riding a white horse.

Captain Pearl is buried in the church yard of the Anglican Cathedral on Duckworth Street in St. John's. The tombstone, one of the few still in the old cemetery, is not on the actual grave of Captain Pearl. Over the years while clearing up the area several tombstones, including Pearl's, were laid on the north west corner of the grounds.

A GARRISON IN THE ATLANTIC

In the early years of colonization, Newfoundland's geographic position made it invaluable to both Britain and France: first as an excellent fishing ground with the opportunity of using the island as a place for curing, storing and shipping fish; secondly for its strategic military position, where troops could be rested, assembled and provisioned to maintain control of North America. From the early days up until the end of World War Two, St. John's played a key military role. Here are a few stories from that interesting past.

HE BEAT THE FRENCH ARMY

Originally appeared in *Jack Fitzgerald's Notebook*

John Earle, his wife and three children, the only inhabitants of Little Bell Island, successfully fended off the French army in 1696 after the French had invaded St. John's and Bell Island. He accomplished this feat through courage and imagination

When Earle learned of the French invasion of St. John's he knew it would only be a matter of weeks before they would invade Bell Island and then Little Bell Island. Although the odds were great, Earle was determined to make a stand to defend his island home. One advantage he had was that there was only one landing spot on the island, which was located on a beach. It was on this beach that

Earle planned to make his stand. He carted a small cannon down the slope and placed it in position.

He then made a dozen or more wooden cutouts that resembled soldiers. Earle constructed a fortress along the beach and placed the wooden soldiers at strategic points along the front of the fortress, placing a musket with each figure. When he ran out of muskets he used wooden sticks carved to resemble muskets.

On January 19, 1697 the French left Portugal Cove, using two long boats to ferry their troops. Earle waited patiently and when the first barge moved into the cove he waited until it got close enough, then fired his cannon and sank the French troop carrier. While the other soldiers were pulling their comrades from the water Earle ran from wooden soldier to wooden soldier firing a musket from each position.

This unexpected resistance on the island convinced the French they were up against a well-trained fighting unit, and they immediately retreated. Little Bell Island, thanks to the courage and ingenuity of John Earle, was the only settlement in Conception Bay not destroyed by the French during the invasion.

John Earle and his family knelt and gave thanks to God for their deliverance from the French threat. The Earle family Bible is preserved at the Newfoundland Museum.

THE LIAR WHO SAVED ST. JOHN'S

Originally appeared in Strange but True Newfoundland Stories

Lying is not a practice generally encouraged, but there was a time in our history when a good liar saved the city of St. John's. This unusual episode from our past is recorded in the papers of Governor Sir James Wallace, and preserved at the Newfoundland Archives.

The year was 1776 and the French were taking advantage of the fact that a large number of British troops were heavily committed to the war with the revolutionists in the American Colonies. They could reasonably assume that other British holdings would be lightly fortified. During this period a large French fleet, under the command of Admiral Richery, appeared outside the narrows at St. John's Harbour, which was fast beccomming stragically important as a naval base. St. John's was defended at the time by only three war vessels and about 600 troops. A boom and chain had been placed across the Narrows to prevent access to shipping.

The French needed to assess the military strength of the city. Rather than risking a major military confrontation at St. John's they choose to capture Bay Bulls, and to interrogate any captured prisoners there about the defence of St. John's.

The French easily captured Bay Bulls, along with many prisoners. Among those taken was the master of a fishing vessel, John Morridge, who appeared to be willing to cooperate with the French. He was taken on board the French ship *Jupiter* and questioned by French officers. He volunteered instructions on the correct route to St. John's by land, but described such hardships and hazards that the French were discouraged. He told them that there were 5000 soldiers guarding St. John's, adding that a sea attack would be impossible because the harbour was fortified with 200 cannons.

The French Admiral considered the information and decided against risking his fleet by attacking St. John's.

When Newfoundland Governor Wallace learned of

John Morridge's role in misleading the French he was delighted, and told and retold the story for years afterwards.

ST. JOHN'S MAN CAPTURED SIOUX CHIEF

Originally appeared in *Strange but True Newfoundland Stories*

Andrew Bulger of St. John's, at age twenty-five, captured the chief of the Sioux Indian tribe on the Mississippi. Bulger was a captain in the Newfoundland Regiment during the American War of 1812. He and major William McKay led an expedition of one hundred men of the Newfoundland Regiment from Fort Mackinaw on the Great Lakes to the Mississippi River, five hundred miles into American territory. It was a long trek and a challenging one for the Newfoundlanders. Bulger, in a letter to Colonel McDougal on December 30, 1814 stated, "Sir, I reached this place on November 30. From the moment of my departure from Green Bay, until my arrival here I experienced every misery in the power of cold and want to inflict. I suffered more, sir, during this voyage than you can imagine, much more than even I have suffered during the whole course of my life before. The morning we left to descend the Wisconsin River it was filled with floating ice and there was not a meal of victuals in any of the boats."

Despite the hardships, the Newfoundland force captured the fort from the Americans at Prairie du Chien, and renamed it Fort Mckay. Bulger returned to Canada that summer; but when the British learned that the Americans were planning to send an expedition to recapture the fort, they chose Bulger to return to command the fort against the attack.

When he arrived he found the fort in a disorderly state. The Indians were acting up; there was a shortage of food;

and some of the soldiers were insubordinate. Bulger quickly whipped the garrison into shape. When a Sioux Indian killed two British citizens, Bulger captured the Sioux chief and held him as a hostage. He persuaded the chief to lead him to the murderer. When the chief came face to face with the killer he told Bulger, "This is the dog that bit you." The Indian brave was tried, found guilty and shot by members of the Newfoundland Regiment. The commander of the British Forces in North America, impressed with Bulger's leadership, confirmed his appointment as commanding officer of Fort McKay.

OUR LAST DUEL

Originally appeared in *Newfoundland Fireside Stories*

Newfoundland's last duel took place on September 25, 1866, between Augustus Healy and Dennis Dooley for the love of a prominent city belle. That encounter took place near Fort Townshend and the seconds were T. Barnham, a buyer at Knowling's on Water Street, and a Mr. Thomas Allan.

The whole event was staged in accordance with protocol; the combatants arrived on time and placed themselves in the hands of their seconds. Fortunately, however, someone had the good sense to remove the bullets from the guns thereby averting injury — except to the pride of Dooley who promptly fainted on the spot at the same time the trigger was squeezed.

Healey stood his ground for several minutes feeling he had won, but Dooley got to his feet and the duo chose to settle the matter with their fists. The fight took place behind Casey's Barn* and Healey emerged the victor. Although he won the battle, he lost the prize. The attractive belle ran off and married someone else. Dooley was left with black eyes and Healey a pair of skinned knuckles.

A ST. JOHN'S PAUL REVERE

Originally appeared in *Amazing Newfoundland Stories*

During the American Civil War, the United States came very close to declaring war on England. The speed and determination of a young man from St. John's prevented that from happening.

During that war England had recognized the government of the Southern States, causing public demands across the North for President Lincoln to declare war on Great Britain. On Saturday night June 12, 1866 the Galway liner *Prince Albert* sailed into St. John's Harbour carrying a crucial message to be delivered as quickly as possible to President Lincoln. The message was that England had changed its American policy. The British had decided to withdraw its recognition of the Confederate Government and to adopt a policy of neutrality. They, aware of the discontent throughout the northern United States, felt this new policy would reverse the public pressures on President Lincoln to declare war on England.

The captain of the *Prince Albert* despaired when he was informed that the telegraph line at St. John's was out of order and all the lines were down from the city to LaManche. The Captain knew well that the fate of two great nations, and millions of people, depended on the message getting to President Lincoln in time.

---

* Some writers say Casey's Barn was adjacent to Fort Townshend. Old maps show Casey's Farm north of Gilbert Street including the Charlton Street area.

Thomas Scanlon, an employee of the telegraph office in St. John's volunteered to take the message by horseback to LaManche in hope that the telegraph office there was still operable. The English captain agreed and urged him to travel, "...swiftly."

Mounting a large black horse Scanlon sped over the stony pathway towards LaManche. Wind and lightening storms had played havoc with the poles and trees along the route, and Scanlon reached a point a few miles from LaManche where it became impossible for the horse to travel any farther. He dismounted, and trusted his horse for safekeeping with a farmer named Paddy Conway.

Scanlon then pushed on by foot over boglands, hills and across streams until he reached a small bay where a ferry was in operation. But here again he ran into delay. The ferry was on the other side of the bay and Scanlon had to borrow a gun from a fisherman and fire it several times to attract the attention of the ferry captain.

The captain heard the shots and responded to Scanlon's plea for help in crossing the bay. If water transportation had not been available, Scanlon would have been forced to travel through thick forest and bog, which would almost certainly have brought failure to his mission. When he finally arrived at LaManche the situation there was also grim. Their telegraph was also out of order. Fortunately, Scanlon, being familiar with telegraph machines, was able to repair it and soon had it working. He sent the message which was relayed from station to station until it finally reached the hands of Abraham Lincoln.

Scanlon, waited until confirmation of delivery of the message was received then returned to St. John's. The news of England's new policy of neutrality was welcomed in Washington, and the determination and struggle of

Thomas Scanlon had succeeded in keeping Lincoln from declaring war on England.

NEWFOUNDLANDER WINS
CONGRESSIONAL MEDAL OF HONOR
Originally appeared in *Jack Fitzgerald's Notebook*

During the 1840s John Neil left St. John's with his family to move to the United States. They first settled in Boston and John went on to join the U.S. Army. Like his fellow St. John's native Michael McCarthy, Neil earned a place in American military history by being awarded the Congressional Medal of Honor.

When the Union forces of Abraham Lincoln initiated a top secret operation aimed at ending the U.S. Civil War, John Neil was one of eight men involved in the operation. The plan was aimed at closing the final Confederate port on the eastern seaboard..

US Congressional Records told the story.

The splendid energy of the Union Navy in blockading a seacoast of nearly 3,500 miles had such effect that a year after the commencement of the war there were practically only two ports open along the whole hostile coast — Charleston, South Carolina and Wilmington, North Carolina. These were the channels through which the Confederates, by means of daring and fast blockade runners, communicated with the outer world and obtained all the supplies and provisions they wanted in exchange for their cotton. It was impossible for the navy to close those two places at the time with the sea forces available and without the co-operation of the army; but the army had its hands full just then in other parts of the theatre of war.

The federal navy eventually blocked Charleston and

the Confederates fell back to Wilmington. On September 22, 1864, Rear Admiral Porter was assigned to command the North Atlantic Squadron of the federal navy. The main objective of his naval strategy was to close Wilmington. If he succeeded, his achievement would hasten the end of the Civil War.

At the mouth of Wilmington Harbour was Fort Fisher, with seventy-five guns mounted behind heavy earth-works. Most of the ships in the federal navy were wooden, which made a direct attack by the squadron a risky propo-sition. An answer to Porter's dilemma came on November 1, 1865, when General Butler boarded the Admiral's flag-ship, with a daring plan to knock out the guns at Fort Fisher. His plan called for 150 tons of gun-powder being placed aboard a vessel, bringing the vessel as close to the fort as possible, and then blowing up the vessel. The General suggested that the tremendous shock would level the fort or at least dismount the guns. In order for the plan to work the entire cargo of dynamite had to be detonated simultaneously.

Admiral Porter ordered the powder and secured an old naval vessel, the *Louisiana,* to carry the explosives. The powder was stored on the vessel in bags and volunteers were requested to participate in the dangerous mission. One of the first to volunteer was a crewman of the *Agawam,* quarter-gunner John Neil of St. John's.

On the night of December 23 the plan went into opera-tion, Admiral Porter made one final change in plan just before it started. Despite expert opinion, he was not con-vinced the clockwork and candle idea would work. He suggested that it would be wise to light some pine-knots in the cabin before abandoning the ship.

With everything in place the eight under the command

of Commander Rhind set sail for Fort Fisher. There was increased tension as the ship slipped into the harbour beneath the enemy guns; they could be blown to kingdom come if detected. When they succeeded in getting below the target they acted swiftly lighting the candles and pine knots. The candles and clockwork were to explode the ship in an hour and a half. Having completed their part of the plan, Rhind and his men slipped into the water and began their treacherous swim to a small boat anchored nearby, out of sight of the fort.

The candle work failed but the pine knots set off an explosion. However, it was about two hours late, and the explosion was not simultaneous. The plan failed although the explosion was terrific, and caused extensive damage to the fort. The next day Porter received a first-hand account of what happened when four Confederate deserters boarded his ship, the *Malvern*.

The heroic deed of the eight men was followed by a heavy naval bombardment of Wilmington. The shot and shell crashed into Fort Fisher at the rate of 115 per minute. An hour and a half into the battle the guns in the fort were silenced. Not a single naval man was injured. Within days the confederate forces surrendered. The strategic Fort Fisher, along with some nearby inlets, were now in the hands of the federal forces. President Lincoln was elated. Out of the thousands of troops involved in that battle at Fort Fisher only a handful of men earned the coveted Congressional Medal of Honor. Among them was John Neil of St. John's.

MEXICAN REVOLUTION AND ST. JOHN'S MEN

Originally appeared in *Amazing Newfoundland Stories*

Jim Baird and Patrick Sweeney of St. John's fought, and were killed while fighting, on the rebel side in the Mexican Revolution of 1911. The duo died in the Battle of Casa Grandes. Baird and Sweeney were two of four Newfoundland mercenaries fighting at the famous battle.

They were enticed to join the Rebel Mexican Army by an offer of $300 monthly and a promise of five thousand acres of land when the government of Porfirio Diez was defeated and replaced by rebel leaders. The leader of the rebels was Francisco Madero, who had been defeated by Diez in the presidential election of 1910. Following that election, Diez ordered the arrest and imprisonment of Madero. When Madero finally got out of prison, he started the revolution that ousted Diez, and Madero himself became President.

Most of Madero's forces were mercenaries who had fought in conflicts all over the world. When things got rough at the Battle of Casa Grandes, the inexperienced Mexicans left the battlefield. The others, including the Newfoundlanders, fought to within forty feet of the federal forces using dynamite and nitroglycerine. The attack came to a stop when a bullet hit a one hundred pound package of dynamite in the saddlebags of the rebel captain. Captain Lloyd, although born in Scotland, lived for some years in Newfoundland before becoming a soldier of fortune.

The two St. John's men Baird and Sweeney were killed and two other Newfoundlanders (Mugford and Carter) injured in the blast. The battle lasted only ninety minutes, with Madero's forces being defeated. Carter and Mugford were carried to safety from the battlefield by their comrades. Although the rebels lost that battle they eventually won the war, and Madero became president. The new president did not honour his promise of land grants to the Mexicans and mercenaries.

Mugford left Mexico for the U.S. but Carter enlisted in the forces of Pancho Villa. He was with Villa while Villa was being hounded by the great U.S. World War One hero, General John J. Pershing. Carter eventually left Villa's forces and again settled down in Mexico City.

TEEN CAPTURES TWO GERMAN SPIES

Originally appeared in *Strange but True Newfoundland Stories*

During World War One a fifteen-year-old boy captured two German spies near the Marconi wireless station at Mount Pearl.* The teen, Bernard Groves, armed with a gun was doing sentry duty at the Marconi station on a cold, but clear winter night. Grove's had no real concern that the enemy would attempt to overtake the station. He was more concerned with pranks his friends might try to play on him. A winter storm had covered the area in a blanket of snow, and Groves felt it was just another routine night for guard duty.

Looking out over the open meadow adjoining the station Groves saw what appeared to be two banks of snow move. His first thoughts were that his buddies were out to play a joke on him. In true military style he shouted, "Halt, who goes there?" He thought he would give them a little scare by firing his rifle as well. At the sound of gunfire, two men in white camouflage sheets suddenly stood up, throw-

---

* This is the area of Mount Pearl currently occupied by Admiralty House.

ing off the sheets and raising their hands in the air as a sign of surrender.

Groves, who was amazed when he realized he had captured two enemy agents, retained his composure and kept the men in gun range until he was able to turn them over to authorities in St. John's. It was later revealed that they had been sent to destroy the Marconi station.

The Germans had been dropped off near Bay Bulls by a submarine under the command of Otto Oppelt, who had some very interesting pre-war connections with Newfoundland. Otto was a powerfully-built German who was brought to St. John's by the Reid family, owners of the Newfoundland Railway, to work as their chauffeur.

The German was known throughout St. John's and most people thought he was a reckless driver — often driving through city streets at ten miles per hour! He was also known throughout the city for his wrestling skills and competed in local contests using the name, "Young Hackenschmit." His most famous match took place at the CLB Armoury on the night of June 30, 1911 when he fought a local named Young Olsen. The referee for the match was another famous Newfoundland boxer, Mike Shallow.

The wrestling bout thrilled the capacity audience with the two evenly matched opponents battling for two and a half hours. It ended when doctors felt Olsen had been injured and was unable to continue. Oppelt was declared the winner.

Oppelt returned to Germany in 1914 when the war broke out.

During the war his assignment was to carry out espionage and sink ships in the North Atlantic. Whenever he sank a ship he would always rescue the crew and passengers and land them safely on Newfoundland's south coast.

It was his knowledge of the Avalon peninsula which enabled him to direct the saboteurs towards the Marconi station.

A picture of young Groves standing with his two prisoners was part of a collection of WWI pictures owned by Harold Murphy of St. John's up until the 1950s.

BRITISH TREASURY IN ST. JOHN'S HARBOUR
Originally appeared in *Strange but True Newfoundland Stories*

A top secret story of World War Two involved the British Treasury and St. John's. In July 1940, two ships moored in St. John's Harbour were carrying a cargo classified as top secret, the contents of which were not revealed until after the war. The cargo was a quarter of a billion dollars, which belonged to the British Treasury.

In 1940 Prime Minister Winston Churchill considered the likelihood of a German invasion in England all but certain. He discussed this with his cabinet, and a decision was made to have a major part of the British treasury sent to Canada for safe keeping. If England did fall, the British had a secret plan to carry on the war from Canada.

Within ten days, a fortune of several billion dollars in gold and securities was ready for transportation to Canada. The first shipment went out successfully on the British cruiser *Emerald*. On July 8 the remainder of the valuable cargo left British ports in five ships, altogether carrying almost two billion dollars in gold.

Four destroyers accompanied the fleet until they were twenty miles from England, out of reach of the German Air Force. Although targets for U-boats, they were all capable of travelling at a high speed.

When the fleet passed through Newfoundland waters,

a ship called the *Batory* developed engine trouble. The Admiral in charge decided that rather than slow down the fleet, making it an easy target for German U-boats, he would send the *Batory* to St. John's for repairs. He assigned the *Bonaventure* to escort her.

On the *Bonaventure* and *Batory* combined, there was a quarter of a billion dollars; and when they ran into a heavy fog as they neared St. John's, the Vice-Admiral on the *Bonaventure* expressed grave concern. They reduced speed and made it to St. John's safely.

At St. John's the *Batory* was repaired and went on to rejoin the treasure carrying fleet at Halifax. From there a heavily guarded train took the fortune to Montreal, where it was placed in the basement of the twenty-four story Sun-Life Assurance Building.

The secret of the *Batory* and *Bonaventure*'s cargo was perhaps the best-kept secret of WWII in Newfoundland. Not even the highest government officials here were aware of it.

THE INVASION OF CUCKHOLD'S COVE

Originally appeared in *Strange but True Newfoundland Stories*

Cuckhold's Cove in the eastern area of St. John's near Quidi Vidi Village was the site of a military experiment which had a profound affect on the outcome of World War Two. However, neither the citizens or military in St. John's were aware of what was happening, and the home defence thought the city was being invaded by the German Navy.

The episode began early one morning in 1942 when an alarm was raised and all military personnel in St. John's were placed on alert. This was in response to the sound of gunfire and explosions, and by fire visible in the skies near Cuckhold's Cove.

While the military scrambled to prepare for the expected invasion, they received an urgent call from the commander of the U.S. Forces at Argentia. He told them there was no need to be concerned. He explained that a top secret weapon had been developed at Argentia and was at that very moment being tested near Cuckhold's Cove.

When the media questioned the military the following day about sounding of the alarm, they were told the alarm had gone off accidentally by a short circuit. This answer satisfied the media but not residents living in the area of Cuckhold's Cove. Residents told of being awakened by terrifying explosions and seeing the sky lit up by bursts of flame. The military explained this away by claiming it was something caused by an electrical storm.

Not until the war ended and top secret documents opened was the truth about the Cuckhold's Cove incident revealed to the public. In 1942 the U.S. was well aware that an invasion of Europe was inevitable. Their scientists had developed a weapon which later helped to defeat Germany, and they were looking for a suitable place to test it.

Keeping in mind the lesson of Dieppe and the knowledge of intended landings, they were seeking some method by which troops could gain a foothold on a beachhead without experiencing heavy casualties. In response to the dilemma, the Americans came up with the famous rocket-firing landing-craft, which at the time was regarded as one of the most effective weapons in warfare. The Americans selected the rough and sometimes stormy coastline near Cuckhold's Cove as the place to test this top secret weapon.

The weapon was towed to Argentia, where Newfoundland workmen under the supervision of U.S. Military technicians assembled it. To test the unknown qualities of the rocket-firing landing-craft, it was decided to sail directly from Argentia to the rendezvous point, which was set at about one mile off the coast of Cuckhold's Cove. For tactical and security reasons, the trial run was scheduled for early morning, with stormy weather approximating weather conditions at Dieppe.

The experiment was a success and the new weapon approved. It proved its usefulness in the D-Day landings at Normandy Beach.

Cyril Butler, who lived in the Cuckhold's Cove area and watched the military experiment that night, later recalled that when he described what he had seen to friends in the city, they would laugh at him and suggest he had too much to drink.

THE BIGGEST MASS COLLISION OF SHIPS IN WORLD HISTORY, AND ITS CONNECTION WITH WWII TOP SECRET

During 1947 many of the Allied Forces Top WWII secrets were declassified. Two involving Newfoundland may have been connected.

During 1942 a large convoy of seventy-six vessels was making its way steadily through a dense fog. One vessel struck an iceberg at around the same time that eight other icebergs were sighted. A general alarm was sounded to warn others in the convoy of the impending danger. Instantly, all vessels in the vicinity turned to avoid collision with the icebergs and the result was the biggest collision of ships in history. Twenty-two vessels collided and one went to the bottom of the Atlantic. Fortunately, there was no loss of life and the convoy continued on its mission. The event was classified as top secret.

A convoy forming up in Halifax Harbour, bound for Great Britian.

Another declassified document of 1947 described the plans to invade North Africa. This secret mission involved the amassing of the biggest squadron of ships ever gathered in convoy in world history. The invasion convoy rendezvoused off Cape Race in 1942. This was the starting point of the Allies mission to invade North Africa. Underlying the importance of the mission was that its failure would have made it impossible for General Montgomery to have defeated Nazi General Rommel at El Alamein. Montgomery's victory there marked a turning point in the war.

The invasion plan included ships, destroyers, transport ships and cargo vessels from ports in Bermuda, United States, Canada and Newfoundland. The rendezvous point was off Cape Race, Newfoundland and the ships left their respective ports at different times to avoid arousing enemy suspicion. By the time all participants had arrived at Cape Race, the invasion fleet was spread out over six hundred miles of the Newfoundland Coast.

Because of the massive size of the invasion convoy and the fact it was in operation the same year as the mass collision of ships, it is very likely that the seventy-six vessels near St. John's Harbour moving in convoy were part of that invasion force.

CANADA'S MOST EMBARRASSING WWII SECRET

The Canadian military's most embarrassing incident during WWII was no doubt an event that took place in St. John's's during 1942. St. John's was a busy port with visiting war ships from many nations, and a likely target for German espionage. The Canadian Forces at St. John's were participants in a special Canadian Security week, aimed at testing Canada's military security both in Newfoundland and across Canada.

A secret known only to the top command of the Canadian Forces involved the staging of an incident to test not only military, but public alertness in the city of St. John's. An unidentified man was dressed in a Nazi Uniform, and his mission was to see how far who could get in the city without being detected. The military was shocked by the outcome.

The Nazi impersonator walked freely around St. John's and socialized without being detected. He stopped people on the streets to ask for directions; visited stores and walked along Water Street and New Gower Street — the city's busiest streets. He found the people very friendly and trusting. However, this shouldn't be too surprising because most people in St. John's had never seen a Nazi uniform.

However, a more startling reaction took place when he visited Winterholme on Rennie's Mill Road, which housed the offices of the Canadian Military Command in St. John's. The Nazi impersonator stopped and chatted with the Sentry's on duty who not only allowed him into the building but left him on his own inside. The impersonator went directly into the office of the Commanding Officer.

In reporting the episode to Ottawa, the Military Commander explained that most people and many soldiers had never seen a Nazi uniform. Just a few months prior to this the British Military held a similar security week. In London they sent two uniformed Nazi impersonators into the streets. The two went undetected for three hours on London streets before being challenged and apprehended by British soldiers.

SOUTHSIDE OIL TANKS TARGET OF "FRIENDLY FIRE"

On Thursday, August 3, 1944 just minutes after the gun on Signal Hill fired to announce to the people of St. John's that the St. John's Regatta was going ahead on schedule; gun fire erupted on St. John's Harbour.

Bullets struck the oil tanks on Southside Hills and sent a work crew on Southside Road scrambling. The incident, which could have caused a catastrophe in the city had the bullets penetrated the tanks, was covered-up and remained a secret until several years after the end of World War II.

The gunfire originated on board the HMS *Dianthus* a Canadian Corvette moored near the Southside of St. John's Harbour. The vessel was scheduled to move out to sea that morning where a drill was to take place to train crewmen on the handling of guns. Despite concern expressed by crewmen, the Captain ordered them to load the Pom Poms (ships guns). In addition to fuel tanks on the Southside, there were many military vessels in port, and some of the crew were worried over the possibility of an accident occurring during the loading process. Their fears became reality.

After the flag went up at Cabot Tower and the Signal Hill gun went off to announce a go for the Regatta rapid gun fire was heard from the Harbour area. While loading the Pom Poms the gun accidentally went off and several of the bullets struck the oil tanks on Southside Hill. Realizing the danger, a crewman from St. John's lowered the gun so it pointed away from the tanks and then shut it down. However, before the gun fire stopped it sprayed gun fire over the heads of men working on repairing the Southside Road. The men scrambled for shelter.

There were no injuries. The *Dianthus* went to sea and completed its practice on schedule.The thousands of city folk at the Regatta that day had no idea how close St. John's had come to a major disaster.

NAZIS AT ST. JOHN'S NARROWS

The people of St. John's were unaware of the danger lying near the St. John's Harbour during the years from 1943 to 1945. The Germans, in an attempt to cut off this port from operations, had laid several dozen highly explosive mines just outside the Narrows.

When the war ended in 1945 a team of British and Canadian minesweeping experts were assigned to remove the mines. One of the two commanding officers of the effort was Lieutenant-Commander James Badcock of Carbonear, the other was Lieutenant-Commander Jack Davis of Saint John, New Brunswick.

Captured German submarine. It was a submarine like this one which laid several dozen mines near the entrance to St. John's harbour.

While serving with the famed Dover-patrol Sweepers during 1940-41, Badcock was injured while disarming a mine, and had the heels of both feet shattered. The injury left him with a limp for the rest of his life.

British documents described the sweeping operations as, "...a very difficult job which was executed with skill and determination by the little ships of the Black Ensign Fleet." The team of experts worked from dawn to dusk for several weeks before successfully completing their mission. The commanders held conferences each night with the men to record progress and iron out difficulties.

The operation used nine British minesweepers to keep main shipping channels from the harbour clear for shipping while the Canadian vessel *Kipawa* placed Dan Layers or buoy markers to identify the mines for the sweepers.

Some of the mines were actually brought to shore and dismantled by Lieutenant George Rundle and Lieutenant Ceaman Wells. Rundle had been awarded the George Medal for mine disposal work when the Nazis made abortive attempts to block off Halifax Harbour in 1942 and 1943.

Rundle and Wells worked up to their waists in water to steer deadly explosives around the rocks and shoals until they arrived safely on shore.

Badcock told reporters, "The wide range of the sweep and deep water made it a tough task. For quite awhile after the mines were originally detected we swept without success, and the men were feeling pretty glum. Then, we got two in one day and their morale soared sky high."

The St. John's *Evening Telegram* noted, "Badcock had the satisfaction of seeing every mine accounted for." His personal papers contain a letter of praise from the British Admiralty. The letter stated, "He displayed gallant conduct in carrying out daily sweeps under fire of the Luftwaffe and shore batteries on the French coast where lanes were cleared for the invasion of France."

NEWSREEL REVEALS SOLDIERS' DEATH

St. John's born William Ellis learned of his brother's violent death in a unique way. His brother, Private Sam Ellis, was fighting with U.S. forces in the South Pacific during 1945. Bill received a letter from Sam in May 1945 in which Sam assured his family he was safe and well. Two days after receiving the letter, Bill rushed home after spending an evening in downtown Newark, New Jersey, and told his family that Sam was in great danger.

This was no premonition, no token, no psychic warning

This is the photo Bill Ellis was able to get from the movie theatre operator in New Jersey. The photo shows Sam Ellis on a stretcher outside the field hospital.

of any kind. Bill had learned of his brother's danger in an unusual way. He was at the movies, watching a newsreel of the Okinawa Campaign, when he recognized a seriously injured soldier being carried from the battlefield as his brother Sam.

The following day Bill went to the theatre manager and requested a replay of the film so he could make a positive identification. The manager obliged, and then gave him several frames of the movie which Bill showed to his family. While the family were discussing the film clip they received a visitor from the War Department. The officer advised them that Sam had died from wounds received on Ie Shima in the Okinawa campaign on April 18, 1945. Sam was forty years old at the time of his death. He had fought in the Leyte, Guam and Okinawa campaigns. He was cited by the U.S. Government for his efforts in evacuating the wounded men from the battlefield under intense fire. For his bravery, Sam Ellis of St. John's, was awarded the Bronze Star, the Medal of Honor and the Purple Heart. An interesting sidebar to this story is that noted war correspondent, Ernie Pyle, was killed in the same battle, on the same day.

Sam moved from St. John's to the U.S. in 1925. After the death of his wife in 1934, Sam sent his son, Joe, to live in St. John's with Mr. and Mrs. Joseph Ellis, (Sam's parents), where he remained until the late 1940s. After returning to the United States Joe served with the U.S. Army in Korea.

ST. JOHN'S WAR HERO

Lieutenant Rupert Jackson, who once served as public relations director in the office of Premier Joey Smallwood, was a distinguished war hero and was awarded the M.B.E. (Member of the British Empire). On February 5, 1945 Jackson entered an area devastated by German artillery — and which had been left heavily booby trapped — to rescue four men. Two were injured and two were unharmed but trapped in the minefield. Jackman led several volunteers who risked their lives in locating and marking the hidden land mines.

His citation read, "he displayed throughout, the utmost coolness and resource and a complete disregard for personal safety. The dangers were well known to all and the weather conditions of this rescue could not have been worse — pitch dark, raining and the ground frozen bound and covered with melting snow. The entire operation

POLITICS, RELIGION AND STRANGE, STRANGE TALES

In *Newfoundland's history politics and religion have often gone either hand in hand or head to head. Newfoundland has had more than its fair share of interesting characters, incidents and 'firsts' in both fields. What follows is a collection of stories from sources such as newspapers of the day and official correspondence, documenting some of the more interesting stories with a St. John's connection.*

GRAVEYARDS
Originally appeared in *Newfoundland Fireside Stories*

From the arrival of Sir Humphrey Gilbert until the end of the eighteenth century the only religion permitted in Newfoundland was the Church of England. Once a Church of England parish had been established in St. John's, an Anglican graveyard was opened. It was located at the site of the present Anglican Cathedral opposite the Court House on Duckworth Street.

The Anglican Church viewed Newfoundland as a mission parish, and the bodies and souls of all the inhabitants were, in theory, property of the Church. Even when other religions were established here, all faiths were expected to bury their dead at the Anglican Cemetery. No religious ceremony was complete without the sanction of Anglican

Some of the old graves still remaining in the cemetery beside the Anglican Cathederal. The furthest one down is that of Captain Pearl. (See "Lady Pearl's Ghost," page 63.)

clergy. Even under the popular Roman Catholic Bishop, Louis O'Donnell, this double-rite system continued.

It meant that baptism, marriage and burial services had to be performed by an Anglican priest in addition to the Roman Catholic priest. When a royal proclamation was issued in 1784 giving freedom of worship to all, the double-rite practice continued in Newfoundland. Roman Catholics often defied the local law and would wait until nightfall to bring their dead into the cemetery to conduct their own services.

Catholics pressured the Newfoundland governors to allow them to have their own graveyard and conduct their own burials. They were told that they could have their own cemetery, but until one was found they would have to continue to use the Anglican cemetery and clergy.

The Catholics established a cemetery of their own in 1811 on a parcel of land at the corner of Long's Hill and

Queen's Road. The site is now occupied by the Presbyterian Kirk. The first person buried there was Mrs. John Butt, whose body was removed from the Anglican Cemetery and re-buried at the Catholic Cemetery. She was ninety-four years of age, and the oldest person in St. John's at the time of her death in 1784.

Tombstones were rarely used in St. John's before the 1820s, but over the following decade many were imported from Waterford, Ireland, a tradition which became widespread. Near the end of the nineteenth century the graves at Long's Hill were moved to make room for road construction and for sanitary reasons. The bodies were transferred to Mount Carmel and Belvedere.

During the process of digging up, the bodies were piled along Livingstone Street. Over the following week a disease spread throughout the neighbourhood causing thirteen deaths.

On July 1, 1849 Governor LeMarchant ordered that all graveyards within St. John's were to be closed. It took several years for the closure of city cemeteries to be completed. On May 25, 1849,* the General Protestant Cemetery on Waterford Bridge Road (then on the outskirts of the city) was opened. On June 25, 1849 the Anglican Cemetery on Forest road was opened.

On June 26, 1855 the Roman Catholics consecrated,

---

* There is some contradictory information regarding this date. While all written references clearly support it, there is the headstone of one John Butt, about halfway along the Topsail Road boundary, stating that he died on 11 May 1842 and was buried on Sunday 15th, and that his was the first burial there. Was the cemetery in unofficial use prior to the 1849 date? Had Mr Butt been previously interred elsewhere and re-interred in the GPC? Was the headstone installed at a much later date, and the information inscribed is in error?

Mount Carmel Cemetery overlooking Quidi Vidi Lake. On July 1, 1855 Belvedere Cemetery was consecrated.

A PRINCE ATTACKS A BISHOP

Originally appeared in *Jack Fitzgerald's Notebook*

The residence of the Roman Catholic Bishop was originally located on Henry Street on the site now occupied by the Star of the Sea Association. Bishop O'Donnell complained to the Governor about Prince William's efforts to hinder development of the Catholic Church in Newfoundland. After being informed by the Governor of the complaint, the Prince (later King William IV) who was living in St. John's at the time, developed open hostility towards the Bishop and frequently insulted him. On one occasion when he was passing the Bishop's residence on Henry Street he tossed an iron file through the palace window. The file struck O'Donnell, almost breaking his shoulder.

O'Donnell learned that the Prince was planning to kill him and claim he was responding to an insult from the Bishop. In addition, he believed the Prince intended to burn down the Catholic Church on Henry Street.

For more than two weeks O'Donnell was forced to hide out in the attic of a friend. Not even the friend's family were aware the Bishop was in the house. Only after Prince William departed Newfoundland shores did O'Donnell come out of hiding.

MRS. TRAVERS LOCKED OUT GOVERNMENT

Originally in *Newfoundland Fireside Stories*

A tavern located at the corner of King's Road and Duck-worth Street, owned by Mary Travers, played a unique role in the political history of Newfoundland. During Newfoundland's first election, in September 1832, the Travers establishment had been used by authorities for voting and other purposes connected with the election.

On December 26, 1832, Travers Tavern became the seat of the Newfoundland Government, with the legislature holding all its sessions there. One of the first items to be discussed by the first legislative session was an appropriation for rent for Mrs. Travers. Although rent was approved, many months passed without it being paid.

At first Mrs. Travers petitioned the House for her rent. When this failed she resorted to legal action. She had the court issue a restraining order and seized the speaker's chair, the cocked hat and sword of the Sergeant-at-Arms, and the books and papers belonging to the legislature. She also took possession of the mace.

Rather than pay their debt to Mary Travers, the legislature moved to new quarters at the old Court House. Meanwhile, Mrs. Travers placed an ad in newspapers announcing she was going to auction the objects taken from the government. The legislature demanded she return the items. But the strong-willed Mrs. Travers refused and threatened to go ahead with the auction. The government finally gave in and paid her the $350.00 she was owed.

A JUDGE IS ARRESTED

A rare occurrence in judicial history took place in St. John's in 1838. A private dispute resulted in a prominent city doctor being imprisoned and the judge and High Sheriff who released him being placed under house arrest. The case had repercussions throughout the British Empire.

The incident took place on August 7, 1838 after John Kent, a member of the House of Assembly, expressed strong criticism of Dr. Kielley's performance at the St. John's Hospital. Kielley's office was on Water Street west of Bishop's Cove near where Templeton's Paint and Hardware operates today. Kent was about a dozen doors east of Kielley's.

Angered by the comment, Kielley sought to bring the matter to court. After outlining his case in a letter, he sent a messenger to deliver it to the Court House. Kielley watched the messenger and, when he passed Kent who was standing in the doorway, shouted orders to show Kent the letter. Dr. Kielley then went to Kent and, angry over statements made in the House, called him a liar and physically threatened him.

Kent retaliated by charging the doctor with violating House privileges by attacking him. Dr. Kielley was summoned to appear before the Bar of the House of Assembly to answer Kent's charges. However, he was not allowed to speak on his own behalf. The Speaker advised him that he could only throw himself on the clemency of the Assembly.

Kielley accepted but instead used the chance to again call Kent a liar. He was found guilty of a breach of privilege and sent to prison. The arrest was made in a ceremonial manner. The Sergeant-at-Arms with mace in hand escorted Kielley to the Duckworth Street prison. Kielley appealed the decision and had it overturned by Judge Lilly. Kielley had argued his dispute was not a matter for the House because it was a private dispute between himself and Kent.

When the Assembly learned off the release of Kielley they ordered the arrest of Judge Lilly and the High Sheriff. By then the episode had become widely known throughout St. John's and crowds gathered near the Duckworth Street Prison. The crowds cheered when the Sergeant-at-Arms arrested the duo and escorted them to serve a sentence of house arrest. The Governor supported the decision of the House, and Kielley appealed the matter to the Privy Council of England.

The Privy Council studied the matter and gave a decision in favour of Dr. Kielley. In doing so they set a precedent in limiting the powers of colonial legislatures throughout the British Empire.

THE BATTLE OF WATER STREET

On the evening of May 13, 1861 Water Street was like a scene out of Dr. Zhivago. Crowds had flowed onto the street and congregated in the area between the Market House (Court House) and McBride's Hill. The Governor, concerned over the rioting at Colonial Building by a mob earlier in the day ordered mounted troops to go to Water Street to disperse the crowd.

Led by Colonel Grant the mounted soldiers made their way down McBride's Hill and formed a line at the intersection of McBride's and Water Street. By the time they arrived violence had already erupted and the mob stormed several stores, smashing windows and looting as they

Water Street, west of Market House, where the riot of 1861 took place.

went. They demolished the premises of Nowlan and Kitchen and burned down the stables of Judge Robson, the Theological Institute and the cottage of Hugh Hoyles. This was followed by an unsuccessful attempt to burn the house of the Anglican Bishop.

In the midst of the outbreak, two prominent citizens tried to persuade the crowd to disperse and go home. Father Jeremiah O'Donnell, who had quieted the mob earlier at Colonial Building; stood in front of the Market House and appealed once more for the mob to listen to him. Judge Little had refused the advice of the military and bravely made his way to the centre of the rioters.

Meanwhile, Grant was trying to reason with the mob near McBride's Hill. Any expectation he had that the military presence would intimidate the rioters was quickly quenched, when he was showered with verbal insults and knocked off his horse.

He managed to climb back on and lead his force on a charge into the crowd. His soldiers fired into the mob and when they finished three men lay dead on the street and four more were wounded.

Around the same time a would be assassin took a position near the Market House and began firing at Father O'Donnell. O'Donnell was shot in the ankle and a man standing next to him was seriously injured. It is believed that the gunfire came from an upstairs side window at O'Brien's Butcher's Store, immediately west of the Market House.

Judge Little appealed to Magistrate Bennett to call off the troops. Bennett refused and insisted the military were needed to protect public property. Little then appealed to Colonel Grant and assured him of peace if he would take his troops and leave. Grant agreed on the condition that Judge Little accompany him and the troops back to the barracks at Fort Townshend.

When Bishop O'Donnell learned of the shootings he ordered the tolling of the Cathedral bells to summon the population to church. The ringing of church bells was a common practice used to call parishioners together during times of crisis. The Cathedral was filled to capacity when Bishop O'Donnell took to the pulpit and gave a fiery condemnation of the violence and rioting. He then ordered the crowd to go to their homes, wash their wounds, and to bury their dead.

The crowds responded and dispersed. Peace returned to the city. Within a month, the butcher O'Brien had sold his building and left Newfoundland. He was never charged with any of the shootings of May 13.

These events in 1861 followed the General Election held that year. Intimidation was rampant, there were beatings, shootings, destruction of property and riots. This lawlessness was inspired by occurrences in the district of

Harbour Main. On polling day, May 2, George Furey, cousin of Government Party candidate Charles Furey, was shot and killed. The returning Officer was so intimidated by threats of violence that when the vote count was completed he refused to make the results known. His fear wasn't alleviated by the presence of fifty members of the Royal Newfoundland Regiment sent into the district to keep the peace on election day.

On May 13, 1861 the House of Assembly met to settle the outcome of the election. The final count in the dual riding of Harbour Maine was Nowlan 325; Byrne 322 and their opponens Hogsett, 316; Furey 310. Hogsett, a lawyer and former Attorney General, insisted on taking a seat in the House even though he had lost the election. the *Times*, published in St. John's, warned that, "A forceable entry may propel the perpetration into quite a different atmosphere to answer the violence."

When Furey and Hogsett took their seats in the legislature they were ordered by the Speaker to leave. Furey left quietly but Hogsett had to be forcefully removed. Kenneth Maclean, a House Member, was attacked by a mob outside Colonial Building as he walked towards the entrance. He managed to break away and outrun his attackers. Another MHA, Hon. P.G. Tessier, was also followed by the mob but managed to gain entrance to the House before they could catch up with him

When the crowds heard that the assembly had refused to allow Hogsett and Furey to take a seat in the legislature they tried to force their way into Colonial Building. The military joined with the police in preventing the mob entry. At this point, Father Jeremiah O'Donnell, a Roman Catholic priest stood on the steps at Colonial Building and successfully persuaded the crowd to disperse peacefully.

However, as they moved away, several men threw punches at Kenneth Maclean who had to be rescued by Father O'Donnell. Hours later the mob reformed and began their assault in the Water Street area.

THE CASE OF THE HEADLESS INDIAN

A grave just east of the old Long Bridge on Southside Road contains the body of the last of the Beothuck Indians of Newfoundland. Buried in the grave is a rather startling secret. Only part of the body of the victim was actually buried. If the grave was opened today we would find that the head had been cut off and removed before burial. Shanawdithit, last of the Beothucks, was buried without her head.

Even more surprising is the fact that the head was surgically removed by a prominent figure of Newfoundland history. Dr. William Carson — instrumental in obtaining Responsible Government for Newfoundland —

The plaque identifying the site of St. Mary's Church on the Southside of St. John's Harbour, and the burial place of Shanawdithit.

Shanawdithit

aware that Shanawdithit was the last of her tribe, removed the girl's head before she was laid to rest. The girl, along with her mother and sister, had been captured in 1823 and taken to St. John's. Her mother and sister passed away soon after. Shanawdithit died in 1829.

Dr. Carson shipped the head to the Royal College of Physicians at London, England where it ended up in a medical museum. During World War Two the Museum was bombed and the Newfoundland artifact was lost forever.

According to archival records Shawnawdithit stayed for awhile in the St. John's home of W.E. Cormack, the first man to walk across Newfoundland. Throughout his trek Cormack made a futile search for Beothuck survivors. He did however, find the remains of a Beothuck village with some evidence of recent habitation. J.R. Smallwood's *Encyclopedia of Newfoundland* notes that Cormack found evidence of the tribe being in a state of starvation. By that time authorities estimated that there were less than thirty Beothuck left in Newfoundland. And these may have already perished through starvation and disease.

Shanawdithit is buried at the site of the old St. Mary's Church on Southside Road. A monument at the site reads in part, "Near this spot is the burying place of Nancy Shanawdithit very probably the last of the Beothucks who died on June 6, 1829.

THE GOLDEN ROSARY BEADS

A set of rosary beads, made from forty nuggets of Klondike gold, played a key role in the founding of St. Clare's Hospital at the corner of St. Clare's Avenue and LeMarchant Road. The hospital, now one of the largest in Newfoundland and Labrador, began in the house located at the eastern corner of the hospital complex.

At the turn of the century this home was privately owned by the Hon. E.M. Jackman, and was known as the 'White House.' In 1913, this house was purchased by the Presentation Sisters from funds raised by Sister Mary Clare (Mary Theresa English of St. John's).

After visiting a home for working girls in Montreal which was owned and operated by the Grey Nuns, Sister Clare returned to St. John's committed to founding a similar facility here. She started a fund-raising effort which involved selling cancelled postage stamps, knitted clothing and public donations.

The former Jackman House, site of the original St. Clare's Mercy Hospital.

James Funchian — a Klondike miner who did well during the 'Gold Rush' — and his wife were friends of Sister Mary Clare. On a visit to St. John's the Funchians gave their friend the set of golden rosary beads. Sister Mary Clare viewed the gift as a blessing from heaven. She sold the special beads to the Knights of Columbus who presented it to Cardinal Gibbons of Baltimore during the celebration of his golden jubilee in the priesthood.

The good sister died before her dream was completed. In 1913 the Presentation Home for Working Girls was opened. It operated until 1922, at which time the Nuns converted it into a hospital which they named St. Clare's, in honour of Sister Mary Clare.

THE BISHOP AND A BRITISH FORTUNE
Originally appeared in *Amazing Newfoundland Stories*

Archbishop Howley, Roman Catholic Bishop of St. John's, had in his possession documents that could have helped a Newfoundland family to lay claim to a fortune in England. However, he refused to share the information.

The fortune, a half million dollars at the time of this story and growing, was left by a Lord Tucker, whose heirs had settled in Newfoundland. Lord Tucker had disinherited his daughter, Lady Alice, because she had married an Irish footman named Pat Molloy against the Lord's will. Molloy took his wife to Newfoundland and settled at Trepassey. When Lord Tucker died, he left his estate to his son who died shortly after. He in turn left his estate to his sister, Lady Alice, whose whereabouts were unknown.

Around the turn of the last century, Archbishop Howley learned of the fortune, and over a number of years compiled a genealogy of the Molloy family in Newfoundland, which proved that Alice Molloy of Trepassey was in fact Lady Alice Tucker. It was Howley's efforts that saved the fortune from reverting to the Crown after going unclaimed for one hundred years.

Following Howley's revelation, people claiming to be heirs of the fortune surfaced all over the world. When Archbishop Howley refused to provide his genealogy charts to any of them, they petitioned the Pope asking him to order the release of the documents.

The Pope replied that he left such matters solely for the bishops to decide. A series of claims appeared in English courts, but no one established legal title to the Estate. During the 1960s, the King family of Cape Breton, Nova Scotia, made claim on the estate and the Trepassey family of John Halleran also claimed to be descendants of Lady Alice Tucker. The estate was never settled.

THAT GOVERNOR

Anti-confederates in St. John's found a creative way to deliver one final insult to Sir Gordon MacDonald, who served as Governor until Newfoundland became a province in 1949. There was little doubt among the anti-confederates that MacDonald was a supporter of Confederation.

In addition to his political bias, MacDonald was considered arrogant and disrespectful of the people of St. John's. While speaking at a church gathering he once referred to "...the winebibbers of the East End and the beer guzzlers of the West End." He forbade the use of alcoholic beverages at Government House receptions.

When he departed St. John's one of his enemies found a creative way to deliver a last insult toward the Governor.

The following acrostic slipped by editors at the *Telegram* and was published on May 8, 1949.

The prayers of countless thousands sent
Heavenwards to speed thy safe return
Ennobled as thou art with duty well performed.
Bringing peace, security and joy
Among the peoples of this New Found Land
So saddened and depressed until your presence
Taught us discern and help decide what's best for
All on whom fortune had not smiled.
Remember if you will the kindness and the love
Devotion and the respect that we the people have for thee.
Farewell!

This clever way to publicly call the governor a bastard is reported to have found its way into the hands of Winston Churchill who was greatly amused.

IRISH CONNECTIONS

*H*ardly *anyplace in the world has closer ties with Ireland than Newfoundland, for although the Irish emigrated to the United States, Canada, Australia and New Zealand, it is in Newfoundland that both the accents and the customs have remained most intact. Here are a few short stories relating to those close ties.*

THE IRISH REBEL

Originally appeared in *Amazing Newfoundland Stories*

Kevin O'Doherty, a famous Irish rebel of the nineteenth century was banished from Ireland and settled in St. John's, Newfoundland. O'Doherty had been captured by the British in 1868 and sentenced to banishment from Ireland for seven years. At the time of sentencing, he was in love with Eva Marie Kelly of Dublin, who was then considered a great Irish poet and referred to as the Poetess of the Nation. When O'Doherty left Ireland Eva was there to promise him that she would wait for his return.

The rebel was put on a ship heading for St. John's, Halifax and Boston and he was given the choice of place to settle. He chose St. John's and assumed a new name. He settled on a piece of land on Topsail Road near Bowring Park, where he lived in a tilt and kept to himself. Local people did not bother him because they believed the tilt he lived in was haunted.

O'Doherty was young, handsome and had a splendid

physique and pleasing personality. He survived by selling the products of the forest and stream, and became well-known around the city as he peddled his goods. Townsfolk considered him a hermit, and had no idea of his true identity.

A written description of the 'Topsail Road Hermit' stated that, "His manner proclaimed the gentlemen, and he would never accept charity, taking money only for the goods for their exact value. Without being melancholy, he seemed to revert to a memory that was not happy, and his habitual appearance kept distant any intimacy that might have been offered."

When the seven-year banishment period came to an end he dressed in fine clothing and jewellery, and boarded a ship for Ireland. Eva Mary Kelly was there waiting for him and the two married. It was not until after his departure that some local Irish inhabitants of St. John's revealed the hermit's identity.

IRISH GUNS HIDDEN AT ST. JOHN'S

Originally appeared in Strange but True Newfoundland Stories

St. John's played a more intriguing role in the Irish opposition to British rule than most people realize. For example, on one occasion Irish rebel forces concealed 50,000 rifles in a field in St. John's.

It was during the mid-nineteenth century, and the Irish rebel movement known as the Fenian Organization had agents assisting them in Newfoundland. Fenian supporters in St. John's helped to smuggle 50,000 rifles, which had been purchased at Portland, Maine, destined for Ireland. The entire operation was top-secret. The St. John's agents unloaded the guns from a ship in St. John's Harbour and buried them in a field located near the home of the Anglican Bishop of Newfoundland.

When a ship had been engaged to carry the weapons to Ireland, the agents removed them from their hiding place and loaded them on board. The cargo safely reached its destination at Kinsale, Ireland.

THE IRA DEATH SQUAD IN ST. JOHN'S
Originally appeared in Jack Fitzgerald's Notebook

An Irish Republican Army death squad once visited St. John's on a secret mission ordered by their leaders in Ireland. Their target, a city resident who at one time was commander of the infamous Black and Tans, a para-military organization sent by British Prime Minister Lloyd George to put down civil unrest in Ireland during the early 1920s.

Sir Hugh Tudor had a lot of military experience and was a lifetime friend of another British Prime Minister, Sir Winston Churchill. When Tudor was wounded during the

Boer War and hospitalized, Churchill sent him a wire saying, "Best wishes for a happy Christmas, swift recovery and all the luck of the war." During WWI, Tudor was commander of the Ninth Scottish division in France, and he is recognized in history as the inventor of the smoke screen used in later warfare.

Major General Sir H.H. Tudor

Unemployed ex-British soldiers, serving as auxiliary

109

members of the Royal Irish Constabulary, made up The Black and Tans. When Tudor's unit was formed there were not enough uniforms to go around and consequently the forces combined parts of the army uniform with parts of the uniform of the Royal Irish Constabulary. Seeing this mixture of khaki and black the Irish quickly dubbed the military force as the Black and Tans, a name referring to the famous pack of Irish hounds. While in Ireland Tudor was also head of the Royal Irish Constabulary, and the Dublin Metropolitan Police Force.

Liam Deasey, a commander of the IRA at that time, later said that Tudor had backed all the excesses of the Black and Tans. When Sir Hugh Tudor retired from service he sought out a place where the IRA were not likely to find him. He moved to Bonavista, Newfoundland and left his wife and two sons in England. He felt they would be safer with him out of the country.

The IRA however, tracked him down after Tudor had moved from Bonavista to St. John's. An IRA court had sentenced Tudor to execution, and the death squad spent several weeks in St. John's developing an assassination plan. This was their first assignment to kill, and they sought the advice of a Catholic priest at the Basilica.

Upon hearing their story, the priest ordered them to leave the country within twenty-four hours or he would report them to local authorities. The squad followed his advice and Sir Hugh was never again bothered by the IRA. On September 25, 1965, at the age of ninety-five and blind, Sir Hugh Tudor passed away. It was ironic that Tudor who held a lifelong hatred for the Irish spent his latter years being cared for by an Irish-Newfoundland housekeeper, Monica McCarthy.

MARINE STORIES AND ODDITIES

No *collection of St. John's stories could be considered complete without including accounts of shipwrecks, courage and survival. This section includes such accounts, as well as a number of oddities and strange occurrences relating to St. John's, and its history as a refuge for ships of all nations.*

INCREDIBLE TWIST

Originally appeared in *Strange but True Newfoundland Stories*

Two vessels, storm-tossed on the North Atlantic, in incidents years apart but travelling identical routes, formed the basis for one of the strangest coincidences in all Newfoundland history.

The strange happening involved Peter Macpherson founder of the Macpherson business at Port de Grave in 1811.

The strange coincidence took place when Peter was returning to Newfoundland accompanied by his aunt after vacationing in England. Their ship was approaching St. John's Harbour; it was so close that Peter could actually see his home in downtown St. John's.

It was at this point that the strange story begins. A sudden wind came up and blew the ship out to sea. The winds increased and caused damage to the ship's mast. When the storm subsided the crew rigged jury masts; but just as they finished, the storm resumed even more fiercely than ever, and blew the ship clear across the Atlantic to the west coast of Ireland.

Meanwhile, people in St. John's who had witnessed the sudden storm and the disappearance of the ship, were convinced it was lost at sea with all hands on board.

While the people in St. John's mourned the tragedy, the passengers and crew were safe in Ireland, waiting for the completion of repairs to their damaged vessel. To pass away the time Peter Macpherson visited some of the Irish cottages in the village. In one of these he saw a painting of a man who was strangely familiar to him. But he didn't know why.

The picture impressed him so much that he asked his aunt to come and view it. She agreed, and when she saw the portrait she gasped and collapsed. When she regained her composure she said, "Why Peter, that's your father." Peter Macpherson was only eight years old when his father died.

When asked where it had come from the portrait's owner replied, "Oh, that washed ashore on the beach packed in a bale of goods. We liked it and hung it up" Peter purchased it, and when the ship was ready for sailing he took it home to Newfoundland. He learned that originally the portrait had been painted in England, and packed in a bale of goods which his father planned to take with him to Newfoundland. His father's vessel set out and followed the same route that young Peter's vessel had taken years later. That vessel also ran into a storm and sank off the coast of Ireland. There were no survivors. Debris from the wreck had washed ashore at the same place Peter's vessel put in at Ireland years later.

Two vessels, storm-tossed, on the same ocean, travelling to the same destination years apart, one lost, the other saved; one with the portrait of the father; the other carrying the son — the odds of them coming together were fantastic. Yet it did happen. The Macpherson portrait did not survive, however. It was destroyed in the great fire that swept St. John' in 1846.

PETTY HARBOUR BAIT SKIFF
Originally appeared in *Newfoundland Fireside Stories*

Petty Harbour, just minutes from St. John's, is among Newfoundland's most scenic communities and has been used in several Hollywood produced movies. One of Newfoundland's finest ballad's, The Petty Harbour Bait Skiff, tells the true story of a tragedy which struck that community on June 8, 1852. The skiff, which carried six people, was returning to Petty Harbour from Conception Bay with a load of bait when, nearly at the entrance of the harbour, a sudden squall took the skiff. She apparently went down stern first, and the only survivors were those who latched onto the jib which remained above water. They were rescued by local fishermen.

Although there were only scanty reports of the incident in local papers, the story was recorded in song by John Grace. The song describes the day the Petty Harbour fishermen set out for Conception Bay. "It was a clear, beautiful summer's day in June with the fields reflecting the many shades of green and valleys in full bloom."

However, by the time they returned, the weather had changed. The wind had increased and heavy squalls were tossing the little fishing craft about in the waters. Grace described it thus, "When we came to the Nor'ad head, a rainbow did appear. There was every indication, that a storm was drawing near. Old Neptune riding on the waves to windward of us lay. You'd think the ocean was on fire, in Petty Harbour Bay."

Grace noted that the Captain's name was John French and second in command was Mick Sullivan. Grace tells in his famous ballad that when news of the tragedy reached St. John's there was crying in the streets.

THE BLACK DEVIL
Originally appeared in *Amazing Newfoundland Stories*

The *Black Devil* was a ship that once frequented the port of St. John's, and was believed to be cursed by Satan himself. The haunted vessel was an all-black cargo ship with the Devil's figure carved on the front. When it landed in port, children stayed away from it and even adults would avoid the wharves after dark.

As with most legends, this one developed from some true happenings during the late nineteenth century. Originally, the ship was one of two left by a wealthy Englishmen to his two sons. The sons got into a heated argument over the name and finally the older one said, "You may call it the Devil if you wish."

"The *Devil* it shall be," the second son replied.

A full-sized figure of Satan was ordered and placed at the bow of the ship. The entire ship was painted black and the word 'Devil' in large gilded letters was painted at several positions on the ship. It was so ominous to see the black ship with Satan's statue sail into port that the story of the Devil ship quickly spread.

It was chartered by John Munn and Co. of Harbour Grace in 1875. The company could not keep a steady crew. Each captain and crew drank heavily and attacked each other with whatever weapons could be found. In 1893,

Captain Patrick Spry* of St. John's took command and delivered a cargo from St. John's to Halifax. Captain Spry described what he claimed was a token which scared the entire crew and left Spry himself shaken. During a moderate wind and rain storm encountered as the *Devil* neared Halifax waters, a man was seen in the mast, standing motionless but holding tight to the rigging. At first Captain Spry thought it was one of his crew members. The man did not respond to the shouting of the crew to attract his attention. When the captain ordered two crew members to go up and persuade the man to come down, the figure turned towards them and they could see his face clearly. Captain Spry shouted, "He's a stowaway." Without warning the man just disappeared, leaving Captain and crew totally bewildered.

The vessel discharged its cargo and began its return to St. John's and the mystery was still being debated by the captain and crew. As the ship passed Renews a stowaway was found in a store room. However, before the captain could question him, he broke clear and climbed the mast. At the top he turned and either jumped or fell into the ocean. His body was never found. When the ship arrived in St. John's, Spry and his entire crew quit, and left no doubt in the public mind that they felt the ship was possessed by the Devil.

Even the elements rebelled against the satanic envoy. Once during a southwest breeze she dragged her anchor and battered Godden's Wharf in St. John's Harbour. Serious damage resulted to the stern and quarterdeck. When

---

* This is the same Captain Spry who painted the picture of the Three Suns over St. John's (see page 18).

she was repaired, the local police ordered the Captain and crew to board the ship and leave port.

The Devil Ship legend was enhanced when the vessel completed a trip from Labrador to England in a record eight days and eight hours. Suspicion gripped the public to the extent that the British Court of Admiralty ordered the owners to change its name. The name was changed to *The Newsboy*.

While on a trip to the Mediterranean, the bad luck ship was caught in a storm and sank. It was replaced by its sister ship, the *Sheiton*, the Chinese name for "Mother of the Devil."

CURSED SHIP

Originally appeared in Newfoundland Fireside Stories

The *Reliance*, a schooner owned by a merchant from Bonavista Bay, operated out of St. John's Harbour for decades. Its crew were mostly St. John's men. Some seamen from the city refused to work on the vessel because of a popular story around town that the vessel was cursed.

The basis of the claim originated when several crewmen from the *Reliance* visited a gypsy at Lunenburg, Nova Scotia, to have their fortunes told. The gypsy told each sailor something which had happened to them in the past with surprising accuracy. So, when she confidently told them that their ship the *Reliance* was haunted by spirits and destined to be lost at sea, the Newfoundland crew abandoned the ship. Over subsequent years the ships' reputation as a haunted vessel spread throughout Newfoundland and Nova Scotia.

The captain however, did not believe in the supernatural or curses and, undeterred, he searched St. John's until he gathered an experienced and fearless crew. They loaded the ship with fish destined for Oporto. But the night before departure the new crew were spooked after witnessing a misty figure of a man at the masthead of the ship. The entire crew quit and the captain had to delay sailing long enough to hire a new crew. Crowds of curious people visited the harbour to get a look at the cursed ship before it set sail.

A week later the *Reliance* was lost at sea, a couple of hundred miles out of St. John's, with all hands on board, The Gypsy's prediction was fulfilled.

GIANT SQUID

Originally appeared in *Amazing Newfoundland Stories*

The waters near St. John's separating the Newfoundland mainland from Bell Island have many secrets. Not the least is the recorded encounters of local fishermen with a sea monster, known as a giant squid, which, up until the mid-twentieth century, was believed not to exist. As a matter of fact, famous U.S. author Charles Berlitz, who wrote the best selling book *Bermuda Triangle* in the early 1970s, claimed there was no actual proof of their existence.

However, throughout Newfoundland history we have many stories of fishermen encountering giant squid. On October 26, 1873 Theophilus Piccott, Dan Squires and Piccott's twelve-year old son Tom,* were fishing off the Bell Island coast when they saw a strange object floating on the water's surface. The trio rowed closer to view the creature and one of the men struck it with an oar. Sud-

---

* Newfoundland Author Robin McGrath recently included this story in her book *Hoist Your Sails and Run*.

denly, the object came to life and rose up out of the water. Its large eyes and long tentacles frightened the men and the young boy. The monster moved closer and began wrapping its tentacles around the dory, dragging it into the sea.

The boy grabbed his hatchet and began chopping off the monster's tentacles. The creature, fell back into the waters and, as it did, it ejected a quantity of inky fluid which darkened the waters. The men estimated that the tentacles were more than ten feet long, and the body about six feet long. It was about five feet in diameter and looked like a monster-size squid.

The fishermen rowed back to shore carrying with them the two tentacles as proof that the giant squid did exist. One of the tentacles was fed to a family dog while the other was sent to Reverend Moses Harvey of Devon Row in St. John's. Harvey was an acknowledged naturalist and someone who might value the object. Harvey wrote to a friend, "I am now in possession of the rarest curiosities in the whole animal kingdom, the veritable arm of the devil fish, about whose existence naturalists have been disputing for centuries. I know that I hold in my hand the key to a great mystery."

An article written by Harvey on the subject was published in the Natural History Society of England's national magazine. He also sent some of the suckers which he cut from its arm. The story attracted world-wide attention, but as the years passed no additional proof was presented and Harvey's discovery was forgotten.

However, during the 1960s proof of the existence of giant squid was recovered from Newfoundland waters. To remove any doubt that they actually exist, one was captured and studied at the Marine Science Laboratory, Logy Bay, by the late Dr. Fred Aldrich, who was the foremost world authority on the elusive sea monster. I was a reporter with the *Daily News* at the time and I attended the press conference where Dr. Aldrich displayed a captured giant squid.

Some years later while visiting Florida I read Berlitz's book and was surprised to read that he was claiming that there was no actual proof of the existence of giant squid. I immediately contacted the famous author and passed on Dr. Aldrich's findings. I received an appreciative response from the author who indicated he would contact the Newfoundland scientist. Dr. Aldrich learned through his studies that giant squid appear in thirty year cycles in Newfoundland waters.

Another story about giant squid took place in September 1877, just four years after the story reported by Theophilus Piccott. In this incident a sea monster, taken from the sea near Catalina, was placed on public display in St. John's. Captain Abe Abbott, who spent his lifetime at sea, in a letter to his son at Boston said, "I have never seen the like of it in my lifetime. Its tentacles are thirty feet long

This is an artist's conception of the giant squid reported by Captain Abe Abbott.

and 5'8" in girth. The body is nine feet long and its girth is 6'2". The circumference of the head is four feet and the tail has a span of 2'9"." Captain Abbott said he heard sailors from around the world talk about these great sea monsters but he didn't believe they existed until he witnessed one himself.

The monster, believed to have been a giant squid, washed ashore during a hurricane gale. It attracted viewers not only from St. John's but the fishing communities near the city. When word of the monster on display spread, people travelled by horse and by boat to witness the wonder.

RATHER FIGHT THAN DIE

Originally appeared in *Newfoundland Fireside Stories*

The year was 1887. The forty-ton cargo vessel *Minnie*, owned by Captain Henry Carew of St. John's, was on its way from Prince Edward Island to St. John's with a load of potatoes when disaster struck. The vessel was just two days out of port when it ran into a blinding snowstorm, accompanied by hurricane force gales. The captain reduced speed to eight knots but, in spite of frantic efforts by the crew to save their ship, the *Minnie* cracked up on Kelly's Shoal off Cape Breton. Five minutes later she partially submerged in shallow water. The crew, Captain Henry Carew, his brother John, Mike Badcock, Pat Gatherall and John Gatherall, were exhausted and frozen but managed to get to shore in a dory and landed at a place called Campbell's Point on Cape Breton, where they literally crawled to shore on hands and knees. The five men soon fell to fighting — but it was no ordinary donnybrook or brawl. The fighting was a creative and desperate attempt by the men to stimulate their muscles and blood flow in order to stay alive.

At first they sought refuge in a wooded area, and came up with the idea to beat each other to keep warm. When they tired of this they set out for a nearby community for help. During this trek, twenty-four year old John Gatherall separated from the group and set out in the direction of a structure that appeared to be a house.

Captain Carew later described their ordeal saying, "It was bitterly cold, and to save ourselves from a similar fate we took to the water. It being much warmer in the water than out of it. We walked in water up to our armpits for a mile and a half, hauling our boat along with us. At the verge of despair we saw a house. This gave us new hope and courage. By then, we were more like moving icebergs than human beings."

The men were welcomed into the home by its occupants and given warm clothing and food. Then the people there joined them in searching for John. John had not gotten very far. He had fallen into a snowbank and frozen to death. The people of the community paid for John's burial. Others were less considerate. They stripped the wreck of all moveable items, including its cargo. Since the *Minnie* carried no insurance, Captain Carew lost everything and returned to St. John's with only the clothes he was wearing.

A HARBOUR CREATURE

Originally appeared in *Jack Fitzgerald's Notebook*

Two fishermen encountered a strange creature outside St. John's Harbour in 1912, similar to the one seen by Sir Richard Whitbourne 150 years earlier. What it was has never been determined but the fishermen — and Sir Richard — were sure it was a mermaid.

The two fishermen said they saw the creature come up from the ocean and try to climb aboard a dory near them. The creature looked around, then came over to their boat and tried to climb into it. The two fought it off and it disappeared into the ocean. The description given in 1912 bore a great similarity to the one described by Sir Richard in his diary. He wrote,

> The creature came to within the length of a long pike from me and was about fifteen feet long. I was standing by the riverside in the Harbour at St. John's when it very swiftly came swimming toward me looking carefully at my face, like a woman. The face seemed to be beautiful and well proportioned. It had about the head many blue streaks resembling hair but it certainly was not hair.
>
> It later came to the boat and put both hands on the side. This frightened the crew and one of them struck it hard on the head causing it to fall back into the water. The men in the boats were frightened by the creature and fled to land.

What was this strange creature? Some suggested it was a seal, but others noted that a master mariner like Whitbourne would know a seal if he saw one. The creature was never identified, but Sir Richard, like the St. John's fishermen of 1912, felt sure he had encountered a mermaid.

NEWFOUNDLAND SEALING SHIP COVER FOR
U.S./ISRAELI INTELLIGENCE

The largest ship in the Newfoundland Sealing fleet sailing out of St. John's Harbour during March, 1947 was the *Mayflower*. The vessel carried a crew of 165 men. Her length was 275 feet; beam 36 feet; draft 17 feet and she weighed 2690 tons. Mysteriously, it was her first and last trip to the hunt. Apart from a ripple of public interest that month the vessel has disappeared from Newfoundland Sealing history.

The *Mayflower* did not end its career in Newfoundland waters because of any sea disaster. After its participation in the 1947 seal hunt, and with faded world interest in it, the vessel went on to get ready for the 1948 secret mission for which it had been prepared.

Before its 1948 participation in a major world event, the *Mayflower* had already earned a place in world history. She was purchased by the U.S. Government on March 19, 1898, from the Ogden Goelet Estate. The ship was built by J & C Thompson at Clydesbank, Scotland, in 1896. On March 24, 1898 she was commissioned at New York and served in the blockade of Cuba during the Spanish American War. She became part of the North Atlantic U.S. Fleet and was the flagship of Admiral Dewey.

In 1902 the *Mayflower* became the official U.S. Presidential Yacht. In 1905 President Theodore Roosevelt U.S.ed the vessel in arranging peace between Russia and Japan . This splendid yacht served Presidents Roosevelt, Taft, Harding and Coolidge. In 1919, for economic reasons, President Coolidge ordered the Mayflower be retired from service.

During 1931, while rusting at the Philadelphia Naval

The USS Mayflower

Yard, the *Mayflower* was partially destroyed by fire. Soon after she was stricken from the U.S. Navy list and sold on October 19,1931. The outbreak of world WWII brought the *Mayflower* into active service again. This time she was refitted and used as a coastal patrol boat for the U.S. Coast Guard.

In 1946 the Americans were secretly involved in helping to organize a plan by world Jewish leaders to return to their homeland in Palestine and establish the nation of Israel. With this end in mind the U.S. Navy outfitted the *Mayflower* to carry Jewish settlers from Europe to Palestine in 1948. Then to divert world attention from the famous ship the Navy sold it to the Shaw Steamship Ltd, who no doubt were party to the top secret operation. In 1947 the *Mayflower,* under the command of Captain Sidney Hill, slipped away from world scrutiny by sailing into

St. John's Harbour during March to join the Newfoundland Sealing fleet.

The following year, 1948, the *Mayflower* was in Europe and ready for its mission. That year the one-time Newfoundland sealing vessel and Presidential Yacht carried Jewish settlers from *Exodus*, a refugee ship that had been forced back from Palestine, and successfully landed passengers at Haifa. The following year the modern state of Israel was founded.

The fate of the *Mayflower* after the success of its mission is unknown.

OUTSTANDING AND
UNUSUAL PEOPLE

St. John's greatest asset has always been its inter-esting and innovative people. They are a people endowed with a 'can do' attitude, and seem to find an opportunity in almost any challenge. The stories in this chapter record but a few of these citizens.

ST. JOHN'S MAN DESCENDANT OF
LADY JANE GREY

William Grey, born at St. John's on April 19, 1850, became the ninth Earl of Stanford. At the time of his death during May 1910, he left a son (Lord Grey Grobyin and Lady Jane Grey living in St. John's). The Grey's were descendants of Lady Jane Grey who served several days as Queen of England. At his time of death Earl Grey was the only born Newfoundlander serving in the British house of Lords. The peerage held by Grey dated from the beginning of the seventeenth century when King James conferred the Bar-ony of Grey of Grobyin upon Sir Henry Grey in 1608. Sir Henry was son of Lord John Grey and the only nephew of the Marquis of Dorset and Duke of Suffolk who was the father of Lady Jane Grey.

The Earldom of Stanford was conferred upon Lord Grey, in spite of the fact his grandfather had been a parliamentary commander during the civil war and one of the judges to sign the warrant for execution of King Char-les I.

THE FRENCH CONNECTION

Originally appeared in Strange but True Newfoundland Stories

The founder of Baine Johnston's Ltd., William Johnston, was a cousin of the French Empress Eugenie, wife of Napoleon III of France. When Johnston made an attempt to visit his cousin in Paris, aides to Napoleon prevented him because they suspected he was a conspirator against the Emperor.

The connection with the French Empress was uncovered by Johnson while researching his family tree. His research also traced a connection to another famous figure in history — El Cid, Campeador of Spain. He established a relationship between his family and the Earl of Fingal, who held the position of British Ambassador to the Spanish Court at Madrid, one of the highest honours given by the Crown at that time.

The Earl's daughter married a Spanish don, a descendant of El Cid. This daughter was a descendant of the Empress Eugenie. While the branch of the Earl's family had died out, the family fortune remained unclaimed in London. Johnston gathered his evidence and set out for Paris to meet with the Empress, to establish the link that would assure both of them a claim to the fortune.

Johnston, with his business connections, had no difficulty in persuading some very influential people to give him letters of introduction to the French court. For a week he was treated well and entertained by members of the French court, who were impressed by his claim to be a relative of the Empress.

But Johnston spoke very little French; and by the end of the week French officials became suspicious. During this period Napoleon had to contend with powerful enemies in his own country.

One newspaper editor so strongly believed Johnston was a conspirator that he refused to help him in any way. Based on these suspicions, Napoleon's aides refused to allow him to see the Empress. Johnston returned to Newfoundland in disgust; but after recovering from his disappointment, he delighted in telling his friends what an unsurmountable difficulty it is, at certain times, to have a friendly chat even with one's cousin's.

CAPTAIN OF THE PRESIDENTIAL GUARD
Originally appeared in Jack Fitzgerald's Notebook

Michael McCarthy, who won the American Congressional Medal of Honor in 1877 and was appointed Captain of the Presidential Guard at the White House, was born at St. John's, Newfoundland and lived in a home on the corner of Gower Street and Victoria Street. McCarthy was born on April 19, 1847. By 1877 he had become a citizen of the United States and a sergeant in the First U.S. Cavalry. Although he was a hero of many battles, his Medal of Honor came from heroism displayed in a savage battle between U.S. troops and the Nez Percé Indians of Idaho.

The ordinarily peaceful Nez Percé sought Government intervention after white settlers took land from them which they had received through a treaty with the U.S. Government. At first it was a battle of words, with both sides seeking support from the government in Washington. Washington sided with the settlers and sent military troops to back them.

Chief Looking Glass, held council with other tribe leaders and agreed to move his people to another site.

While the Indians prepared to move, some white settlers became impatient and began annoying them. A settler deliberately shot and killed a Nez Percé warrior. This shot ignited the smouldering discontent among members of the tribe, and sparked open rebellion. The Nez Percé became as violent and valiant a foe as was ever encountered by any American soldier.

Their first act of aggression was the revenge killing of the brother of the white settler who killed their tribe member. Fearing a massacre the settlers again sought and obtained support from Washington. Meanwhile the Indians had left their reservation and headed northeast towards Montana. They were pursued by the U.S. Cavalry, which had orders to force the Indians back to their reservation. Captain Perry, leader of the cavalry unit did not anticipate the Nez Percé determination to fight the white man if necessary. He felt a show of force would be enough to bring the tribe into submission. Consequently, when his ninety-man party left Fort Lapwai they were poorly equipped. They had only forty rounds of ammunition for their single carbine and twelve bullets for each pistol.

When the troops caught up with Looking Glass at White Bird Canyon, Captain Perry was caught by surprise. The Indians occupied a strong position and indicated that they had no intention of surrendering. A battle was inevitable. The result was the Battle of White Bird Canyon on June 17, 1877. It saw the defeat of the U.S. Cavalry, and Sergeant McCarthy being awarded the Congressional Medal of Honor.

The cavalry were outnumbered eight to one. In addition, they were in an untenable position. Perry noticed that to his right was an elevation of rocky ground and sent

Sgt. McCarthy with a detail of six soldiers to take the position and hold it at all costs.

U.S. Congressional records described the battle:

> Now the fight began. The Indians broke forth, yelling, screaming, filling the air with hideous howls and showers of bullets. As soon as this rush was made it looked as though Hades itself had been turned loose. Eight citizens; settlers who had been most loud in their denunciation of the Nez Percé and their demands for vengeance, took to their heels and ran away as fast as they could. The soldiers too were not prepared to meet this furious and awe-inspiring onslaught and wavered. Soon most the men of 'F' Troop were hurrying to the rear.
>
> Captain Perry, doubting the advisability of the defence, ordered a general retreat. Captain Trimble felt Perry was making a big mistake. He galloped to the commanding officer and pleaded with him to recall the order. He asked, "What is to become of McCarthy and his men. They are in a strong position. If we reinforce him and hold ground there, we shall check the attack." Captain Perry was impressed with Trimble's spirit and argument. He reversed his order. Trimble personally led the men back into battle, but there was still confusion in the ranks.

McCarthy noticed the cavalry's change in tactics and hurriedly rode from his position to assist his captain in steadying the men. Once the attack was properly organized, he joined his faithful six men at the former post. The new burst of courage and enthusiastic fighting by the cavalry was not enough to withstand the onslaught of the overwhelming Nez Percé force. Congressional records describe the scene.

Once more the troops retreated before the exultant

Nez Percé, galloping to some hills which promised protection about a mile away. Their retreat was much faster than the Indians were able to follow. This second retreat left McCarthy and his detail in a serious plight. Completely surrounded by savages he nobly and heroically held his position against the storming foe.

The struggle was observed by his comrades on the hills, who followed every phase of it with anticipations of awe and terror. Closer and closer the Indians drew their circle around the gallant little band. One could now see them shoot, strike or club the foremost of the redskins. Now it was a hand-to-hand fight. Now McCarthy and his comrades could no longer be seen. They were swallowed up the hordes of screaming Indians. The soldiers who were watching from the hill and witnessing the hand to hand battle turned away, sickened by the sight. But again, the figure of McCarthy and his little party sprung up in the middle of the tribe. The gallant little band was cutting its way through the hostilities.

With the odds against him, Lt. W.R. Parnell, inspired by the sight of McCarthy's courage, led a detachment of cavalry to help the battling Newfoundlander. McCarthy fought his way through the Indians and joined up with Parnell and his men. Two of McCarthy's men, however, died bravely during the brief but savage ride.

Parnell's second attempt to battle the Indians resulted in a hasty retreat. McCarthy however ignored the retreat order and without regard for his personal safety continued to battle. He rescued a wounded comrade who had fallen from his horse and encouraged the few men who remained at his side. When his own horse was shot out from under him, he quickly mounted another and slowly guided his men back to the rest of his company. During this retreat his horse was shot from under him again; and in the chaos that followed he became separated from his men.

McCarthy remained cool while in the midst of great personal danger. He saw a clump of bushes behind the Indians, and hid among them. He could see the victorious Indians ride by following his men who were running for their lives. He realized the battle was over and his troop had been humiliated by the Nez Percé.

Nearby lay the body of his close friend; but before he had a chance to hide it, a number of squaws came up and began mutilating the body and removing the dead man's clothing. When he noticed his own boots were sticking outside the bushes and the squaws were coming for them he slipped out of them and withdrew further into the woods. This was enough to fool the Indian women, who believed some soldier must have left them during a quick retreat.

Hours later when things had settled down, McCarthy, bootless and with an empty gun, made his escape by crawling down the bed of the creek and finally reaching the timbered mountains some miles away. From there he wandered over rough territory which caused agonizing pain to his feet.

The St. John's man hid by day, and travelled by night, living on the scant rations he had with him. After continuous hardships, he arrived at his camp at Mount Idaho, thoroughly exhausted. His safe return caused great rejoicing.

Military leaders carefully documented McCarthy's behaviour and forwarded their recommendation to Washington that he be awarded the Congressional Medal of Honor. In addition to being awarded the Medal of Honor, McCarthy from Gower Street, St. John's was promoted to Captain of the Presidential Guard at the U.S. White House.

ST. JOHN'S MAN IN U.S. WHITE HOUSE

John McGrath of St. John's served as personal secretary to U.S. President Theodore Roosevelt. McGrath was born in 1892 and educated at St. Bon's College in St. John's. His experience living in St. John's prepared him well for his work with Roosevelt. While in his early teens, he served as a shorthand reporter with the staff of the Newfoundland House of Assembly. After winning the Jubilee Scholarship and scoring the highest marks in his class, McGrath went on to attend Dalhousie University.

McGrath served the U.S. President until Roosevelt retired from political life. He travelled with the president and got to know the major political and business personalities in the U.S. When Roosevelt retired, George Perkins, a friend of the President, appointed McGrath as manager of his large fish company. He eventually became a partner and when Perkins passed away McGrath expanded the operation to include several other large plants from New York to Lockport, Maine. He was planning further expansion when he passed away on February 18, 1924 at Boston. He left a sister, Betty, and two brothers, Richard and James, living in St. John's. His brother James McGrath served as Minister of Health in the Smallwood Administration. His father was a legislative member and also served as Governor of Her Majesty's Penitentiary.

BIG IN BERMUDA

Originally appeared in *Newfoundland Fireside Stories*

John Pierce Hand was born of Newfoundland parents in Portsmouth, New Hampshsire. However, he grew up in St. John's, Newfoundland and was educated at St. Patrick's Hall School on Bonaventure Avenue. Hand became a legendary figure in Bermuda one of the world's most popular vacation resorts.

John Hand played a major role in developing Bermuda into the great tourist resort it is today. He founded a number of successful businesses there including the Hotel Inverurie, the Hotel Franscatia, the Belmont Manor and Golf Club and the Smoke Shop. In addition, he ran the island's largest real estate firm.

Hand dropped out of school in St. John's during 1898 and took a job as private secretary to Sir Joseph Outerbridge. It was Sir Joseph who introduced young Hand to Bermuda.

When Hand came down with tuberculosis, he moved to North Carolina where the drier climate contributed to his recovery. Outerbridge then sent him to manage the Bermuda branch office of the Outerbridge-owned Harvey and Company. By 1903 he was co-owner of the firm and by 1907, he had formed J.P. Hand Company, with branches in Port au Spain, Trinidad, and Kingston, Jamaica.

He founded the Chamber of Commerce of Bermuda and served as well as chairman of Bermuda's Board of Trade. He is credited with developing the tourist trade from nothing at the end of World War One, to 70,000 visitors annually by 1931, and the industry never stopped growing.

Throughout his successful career Hand never forgot his home in Newfoundland. Every year, from 1920 to his death in 1933, he sent $500 to St. Patrick's Hall Boy's School. He also throughout his lifetime continued his childhood friendship with Mike Ryall, a fellow student of Hand's at St. Patrick's Hall. He frequently sent gifts to Ryall and his family, and paid for many Ryall family trips to visit him at his Bermuda estate. When Ryall passed away during the early 1940s Hand paid for a tombstone to be placed on his friend's grave. Hand's father John B. Hand is buried at Belvedere Cemetery in St. John's, however, J.P was buried at Bermuda.

FLORENCE NIGHTINGALE OF ST. JOHN'S

Originally appeared in *Amazing Newfoundland Stories*

Ethel Dickenson

There is a monument on Cavendish Square, near Hotel Newfoundland in St. John's, dedicated to the memory of the city's Florence Nightingale, Ethel Dickinson who passed away on October 26, 1918.

An epidemic of the Spanish flu began sweeping the world during the last year of World War One, killing an estimated 20,000,000 people. When the epidemic struck St. John's, Ethel was among the first volunteers to provide medical help for the victims. On October 1, 1918, newspaper headlines read: "Spanish Flu Strikes Town." Hundreds of cases were reported. All public gatherings were prohibited and public places closed. Due to overcrowding in city hospitals caused by the flu, the King George V Institute was taken over and used as a hospital.

Ethel Dickenson laboured there day and night, and after two weeks also became a victim of the deadly flu. She had gotten the disease while accompanying patients to the emergency hospital in the old horse-drawn ambulance when she had left her protective nose and mouth gauze behind. Within days she was dead. Health regulations at that time required victims of the epidemic to be buried immediately. Ethel Dickinson was buried that same afternoon. She was thirty-nine years old. Two weeks later the epidemic had passed, and the ban on public gathering lifted.

Ethel Dickenson was the niece of city merchant James Pitts, from whom Pitts Memorial Drive got its name. She was educated at the Methodist College and earned a teaching certificate in Chicago. During World War One she went to Europe as a volunteer in the auxiliary division of the armed forces, and devoted three years to nursing the sick in France and Flanders. When she returned to St. John's she resumed teaching at Holloway School on Long's Hill until the Spanish Flu struck.

Miss Dickenson was the only member of the medical profession in Newfoundland to die from the disease. She became an instant Newfoundland heroine. The people of St. John's showed their appreciation of the work of Ethel Dickinson by erecting a monument in her memory at Cavendish Square.

ALCOCK AND BROWN
PRACTICAL JOKERS

Originally appeared in *Newfoundland Fireside Stories*

Alcock and Brown are remembered as the first men to fly non-stop across the Atlantic. What may surprise most Newfoundlanders is that the two great men were also great practical jokers. While in St. John's preparing for their historic flight, they stayed at the Cochrane Hotel,

Although both Alcock and Brown enjoyed practical jokes, they were quite serious about their work. They are seen here checking out their aircraft prior to departure.

where management threatened them several times with eviction, even suggesting a police arrest if the duo did not stop their practical joking.

On one occasion, following an argument with the hotel cook, Brown, dressed only in underwear, climbed to the roof and Alcock sent up pillow slips which he had tied together forming a rope. Brown stuffed these down the chimney and scurried back to his room.

Not only was the cook forced to leave the kitchen because of thick heavy smoke, everyone in the hotel had to be evacuated. When the commotion caused by the jokers had settled down, the duo started a pillow fight that involved almost everyone in the hotel. Hotel management called in the police to settle things down. The final straw came when just before their famous flight they asked for a tour of the kitchen. It was just after lunch and the staff was cleaning up. Alcock knocked over a pan onto the floor and while the staff was distracted Brown dropped a handful of pepper on the hot stove.

Within minutes after the two left the kitchen, the staff came running out coughing and rubbing their eyes, as the hot pepper spread a mist throughout the kitchen and downstairs area. This time the hotel manager bluntly told them that one more practical joke and he would boot them out of the hotel. It worked.

A monument commemorating the flight of Alcock and Brown was placed in London's Heathrow Airport in 1954.

BOSTON'S MORAN SQUARE
ST. JOHN'S CONNECTION

Moran Square in Boston, Massachusetts, is named in honour of the son of James Moran and Anna (Parrell) Moran of St. John's. The Moran's moved from St. John's to Boston during the mid-1920s and soon after Leonard was born. On January 7, 1954 Leonard, then a sergeant in the U.S. Army and a veteran of the Korean War, lost his life while performing a heroic act. His act of heroism made national headlines in the United States and Moran was posthumously awarded the Congressional Medal of Honor by President Dwight Eisenhower.

On January 7, 1954 Sgt. Moran was instructing recruits at Fort Dix, New Jersey in the handling of grenades. When one of the grenades accidentally exploded in a trench, Moran shielded a young recruit by jumping on top of him and acting as a human shield.

Sgt. Moran was rushed to the army hospital where doctors fought in vain to save his life. He survived only an hour. Meanwhile, the recruit, twenty-one-year-old, Private John D. O'Callighan of New York City received only a flesh wound to the right thigh. The inquiry into the tragedy determined that, "O'Callighan had attempted to throw a grenade out of the trench in which he and Moran were stationed on the grenade range. The grenade hit the parapet and rolled back into the trench. Moran used his body to shield O'Callighan from the blast. In doing so, he gave up his own life."

A shocked and grateful O'Callighan told the inquiry, "...when I tossed the grenade I fell to the ground as instructed but I apparently threw it too low and it hit the parapet. Next thing I knew Sergeant Moran was on top of me covering my body. About the same time I heard an explosion. Sergeant Moran undoubtedly saved my life, but I hate to think of what happened."

This was not the first act of heroism displayed by Moran. While in Korea he saved the life of John F. Norton. Norton told reporters, "Moran threw me to the ground and shielded me while a hail of bullets whirled over our heads.

At its first meeting after Moran's death the Boston South Council named a square in Boston, Moran Square, to honour the heroic marine.

BIG LOUIS BREEN OF FLOWER HILL
Originally appeared in *Jack Fitzgerald's Notebook*

Louis Breen, of Flower Hill, became a real life hero in one of the biggest Hollywood movie disasters in history. During March, 1931, a Paramount movie crew took the dynamite on board the *Viking* which later exploded causing the deaths of thirty-three men, including all but one of the Hollywood crew.

Varrick Frissell* had already filmed the movie *White Thunder*, which dealt with the seal hunt off Newfoundland's coast. However the brass at Paramount felt the picture needed more action scenes in order to increase box-office attraction. As a result Frissell planned a return to northern Newfoundland waters to film an iceberg overturning. To create this scene he planned to use dynamite.

On the evening of the disaster Frissell and his friends were discussing a book entitled *Vikings of the North,* which dealt with the dangers faced by men at sea. As the men discussed the book Frissell told the others that the dynamite they had brought on board was poorly stored in the hallways. At the suggestion of one of the crew members Frissell took it upon himself to make a sign which read 'Danger-Explosives.' He intended hanging this outside the storage room in the hall which housed the bulk of the dynamite. He never finished the sign. Midway though the voyage an explosion rocked the ship, and Frissell was blown overboard. His remains were never recovered.

Louis Breen was a member of the *Viking* crew. He had been to the ice many times before and was a veteran of hardship. The ship was quickly abandoned. But when it became apparent that they would be left on the ice with no food or warm clothing Breen went into action. He led a band of six men back on board the burning inferno. With flames shooting into the dark night sky and the *Viking* still being rocked by explosions, Breen systematically gathered supplies and provisions to help the surviving crew who

---

* Frissell is the spellingused by the *New York Times* and the *New York Mirror* in their reports of the incident. A variety of spellings exist in various accounts of the tragedy.

were then stranded on the ice. He gathered food, burlap to wrap the injured, and cut off the dories which were used to carry the injured to safety.

Louis Breen and his men got off the ship without any injuries, then assisted in placing the injured in the dories. They tied rope to the dories and organized groups of men to drag them over ten miles of broken ice until they reached the safety of Horse Islands. Breen's feet became frostbitten and he later had his toes amputated. Bowring Brothers Ltd. presented Louis with a small cash bonus for his heroism but no other recognition was bestowed upon him.

Over the years the press always found willing survivors of the disaster for their anniversary pieces, but Breen was never contacted. In time the real hero of the *Viking* Disaster was forgotten. Breen himself, never talked about the experience, and in the 1950s moved to Toronto where he passed away.

The Viking

THE REAL 'HAWK'

A popular TV series of the 1980s featured a fictional character called the 'Hawk'! The nickname 'Hawk' really belongs to another hero from downtown St. John's — Jim Lundrigan, a former member of Canada's famous military sky diving team, The Sky Hawks.*

Lundrigan possessed most of the characteristics of the TV Hawk, and shared some similar real-life experiences. Like the fictional Hawk, Lundrigan was cunning and fearless, and a true crime-fighter. He routinely risked his life as a sky diver and also earned province-wide acclaim in British Columbia for capturing a bank robber wanted on a Canada-wide arrest warrant. As if that were not enough, in the year 2000 — at age sixty-three — Jim 'The Hawk' Lundrigan, travelled across Canada and several States, sky diving at every opportunity.

The Hawk, was born in St. John's in 1937, and left in the mid 1950s for a career with the Canadian Army. His plucky, dauntless personality made him a natural for the Army paratroopers division. Lundrigan embraced sky diving with enthusiastic dedication and soon earned a place with the famous military sky diving team, The Sky Hawks.

In retirement Lundrigan was employed by the British Columbia Corps of Commissionaires as a guard at the Toronto-Dominion Bank on Granville and Pender Street. His military training and background prepared him well for the job.

Soon after starting work Jim worked out a signal

---

* The Sky Hawks travel all over Canada performing sky diving shows, during which they perform intricate and death-defying aerial manoeuvres thousands of feet above the ground.

The Sky Hawkes unfurling flags in free fall. Jim Lundrigan is the one on the left, holding the Red Ensign.

system with bank staff to silently alert him if a robbery was in progress. On November 2, 1999, Jim was chatting with a customer when he picked up on a signal given by a bank employee. A robber had quietly passed the teller a note demanding she place all her cash into a bag and pass it back to him. The teller complied. The man then quietly turned, bag in hand, and was moving swiftly towards the front exit when Jim picked up on the signal of robbery.

Without hesitation the Hawk moved swiftly towards the escaping robber. The size of the robber, who was in his late twenties, about six foot tall and 250 pounds, did not deter Lundrigan. In no time the robber was forced to the ground and placed in a head and arm lock. After warning him not to move a muscle, the Hawk carefully read him his rights then placed him under arrest. He then took his prisoner to the managers office. Because at that point it was not known if the robber was carrying a weapon,

Lundrigan advised the manager and staff to stay outside the room while he conducted a weapons search.

During the search several plainclothes policemen rushed into the bank with guns drawn. One, coincidentally, had been in the Canadian army with Jim Lundrigan and when he recognized his old friend he told the others, "Put away your guns boys, Lundrigan got it under control." Police had taken only sixty-seven seconds to respond to the alarm from the bank. When the officers took the prisoner to the police station and checked his identification they learned he was wanted on a Canada-wide arrest warrant.

After retiring from the military the Hawk continued to practice his favourite sport — sky diving. On several occasions during the famous Polar Bear Swim on January first at Vancouver, the Hawk parachuted from an airplane into the ocean to greet the swimmers. He had an unscheduled brush with death on one occasion when a party of sky divers, not knowing Lundrigan's background invited him to join them. One of the divers had a spare parachute which he loaned the Hawk. However, before putting it on, Lundrigan asked several pointed questions about the make, style and how it had been packed. The answers suggested to him that all was in order.

While the owner of the chute was certain it was perfectly safe to use, he neglected to say how long it had been since the chute was last used. As it turned out, the chute had been stored for some time and moisture inside the trunk of the car where it had been stored caused the metal parts of it to rust.

At several thousand feet above ground the sky divers jumped from the plane. All the chutes were opening but it was apparent that something was wrong with the Hawk's chute. He had pulled the rip cord and the chute spiralled out, became entangled, and did not open. To complicate matters the Hawk's left hand became entangled in the dangling chute leaving only his right hand free. He made several attempts to correct the problem but with time running out and the ground getting closer, he decided to pull the rip cord on his emergency chute. But again he ran into problems. He pulled and pulled on the rip cord but got no response. Finally, within a hundred feet of a tree top he pulled the cord with all his might and the chute opened. By then he was too close to the ground for the chute to do anything but slow his descent. Two things saved him that day. The tree which slowed his fall and the fact that a farmer had sprayed his field hours before. The Hawk's fall was cushioned by about six to eight inches of mud.

Within minutes the others came running towards him certain he was either dead or badly injured. Just as rapidly an ambulance sped towards the downed sky diver, Lundrigan stood up, brushed himself off and refused to go in the ambulance. When he inspected the chute he noticed the metal parts which had rusted. After cautioning the other sky divers about the need for closer attention in packing and storing chutes, he brushed the mud off himself and walked away.

After such a close brush with death most men would never return to sky diving, but not the Hawk. Two weeks later he was again jumping from a plane just miles from Vancouver Island. He never lost his nerve and insists he will continue to sky dive until health or death stops him. I last spoke with the Hawk on August 30, 2000. He expressed his love for sky diving and hopes that when his number is up it will come when diving from a plane. As he left he turned, extended his hand to shake mine and said, "See ya in hell."

THE MATADOR IS A LADY

Originally appeared in *Newfoundland Fireside Stories*

St. John's born Carolyn Hayward has a unique position in Newfoundland history. Hayward was an internationally acclaimed professional bullfighter. She was born in St. John's in 1927 and moved to Toronto after graduating from Bishop Spencer College.

Her interest in bullfighting began in 1957 while vacationing in Spain and that same year she fought her first non-professional fight at Plaza de Toros in Toledo, Spain. While there, she met a man who helped and encouraged her to pursue a career as a professional bullfighter. He was Miguel Anegel Garcia, a famous Mexican matador. Garcia suggested to Carolyn that she go to Mexico to train as a bullfighter.

Carolyn, certainly an adventurous and fearless type, returned to Canada in 1958 and, a month later, moved to Mexico to begin her career as a professional bullfighter.

One year later she signed her first contract. The event had been arranged by Garcia. Her first fights took place in villages throughout Mexico with her first major battle at Medida, Mucatan, Mexico. In 1961 she defeated two world-renowned bullfighters: Patricia Hayes, a Texan and Magdalena Azpota, a Columbian. After winning that fight, she cut off the bull's ears and the cheering, enthusiastic spectators carried her on their shoulders out of the ring.

Hayward's fame spread throughout South America, Spain, the U.S. and Canada. She appeared on the popular Canadian shows *Front Page Challenge*, *What's My Line* and *I've Got a Secret*. The Canadian Broadcasting Corporation produced a documentary on this Newfoundland bullfighter in 1963.

Hayward retired from her profession in the 1970s and enrolled at the Cultural Institute in Lima, Peru, to study art. Since then she has become a successful artist in Peru, and has held a series of very popular art exhibitions in Peru and California.

QUEEN OF THE BOWERY

A woman, famous in New York State as Queen of the Bowery, married a St. John's sailor and settled down to live in the city of St. John's, Newfoundland. The wedding was covered by the New York *Daily Mirror* and the following account appeared in that paper on May 22, 1952.

The article stated,

> The blue bloods of hobodum turned out in masses yesterday for the Bowery's biggest social event in years — the wedding of their cigar smoking Queen, Box-Car-Betty. She was also known as Queen of the Hobos, a title earned because of the thousands of miles she travelled all over America in railway box cars during the heydays of hoboism.

This magnificent event in the Bowery of New York City had a close relationship to Newfoundland because the man Box-Car-Betty married was a St. John's globetrotting sailor named Christopher Luby. The newspaper noted,

> Betty fetchingly attired in a blue suit and a beret to match, and Christopher wearing an open neck shirt, a blue sweater and a cap were spliced in a single ring ceremony at the Municipal Building. A nuptial breakfast followed in a Chinatown restaurant, after which a formal reception with cigars, beer and scotch for all was held in the office of the *Bowery News*, which employed the bride as beauty editor.

Luby gave his bride a sparkling diamond ring and a shoulder bag he purchased while visiting Egypt. Box-Car-Betty's real name was Emma Bertha Link and she was fifty-five years old at the time of the wedding. She told friends she would open a boarding house in St. John's. The newspaper lamented, " The Bowery will never be the same without Box-Car-Betty."

Nothing more is known of Box-Car-Betty. Whether or not she achieved her goal of opening a boarding house in St. John's has not been documented.

BART WENT OVER THE MOUNTAIN ... FOR CHICKEN

One of the most remarkable legends of St. John's is the claim that a young City man drove his car over a 300 foot high cliff at Outer Cove to risk his life for a bucket of Kentucky Fried Chicken. The story began after twenty-two year old Bart Connors was rescued from the Outer Cove Beach below Look Out Point by an RCMP rescue team, after surviving driving over the cliff. The story quickly spread throughout the City and eventually T-Shirts appeared with the printed message: "Bart Went Over The Mountain" on front, and on the reverse side "For a Bucket of Kentucky Fried Chicken."

Bart accepted the out-of-control legend with good humour and at one time wore his own T-Shirt with the printing limited to Bart Went over The Mountain. I interviewed Bart on March 14, 2001 and he welcomed the opportunity to set the record straight. Although, the bucket of chicken story is not true, the real story is just as incredible. Bart Connors, is believed to be the only person to crash a car over the near 300 foot drop at Look Out Point, and live to tell the tale.

The near tragedy occurred at night on June 30, 1979. At around 11:30 p.m. Bart Connors was speeding up the road towards Look Out Point. A thick fog had engulfed the area but Bart felt confident he could handle the car under the circumstances. He said, "Although it was foggy I was speeding. There was a guard rail in place but I did not see it. When I tried to take the turn I missed the guard rail by a few feet and thought I was going off the road. Instead, I was heading out over Look Out Point. The car took the top part of a tree at the edge of the cliff right off."

The thought of impending death did not enter his mind as the car descended in a free fall towards the beach. He recalled, "I remember the crash and I remained conscious. I was crying out for help." Then a sound penetrated the silent night air that caused Bart to fear for his life. He said, "I heard the sound of the water moving up the beach. I was trapped in the car and I thought that the tide was rising. I worried that the water would cover the car with me trapped inside."

Meanwhile, a crowd had gathered up on the cliff and the RCMP had been notified. An RCMP rescue boat neared the scene around the same time that a local fisherman moved into the area to attempt a rescue. The fisherman got into trouble and his boat struck a rock and sank. The fisherman made it safely to the beach.

Bart recalled, "I heard a voice say, 'You better bring a body bag.' I knew they were talking about me." The police were amazed when they reached the wreck and discovered that Bart Connors had survived the crash. He was taken from the wreck and placed aboard the rescue craft. Within twenty minutes he was in the care of doctors at the Health Science Centre.

"The outlook was not good," Bart remembered. He said,

"The doctors examined me and commented that I might never walk again." But once again Bart Connors beat the odds. He recovered with only injuries to his knee and leg and within two weeks was released from hospital. Memories of his close brush with death have never bothered Bart. He said he put the episode behind him and went on with his life.

Bart has no idea as to who started the bucket of chicken rumours. He concluded, "It doesn't bother me anymore. I know the truth about what happened and that's enough for me."